I Want to Teach my CHiLD About Manners

BY

JENNIE BISHOP

Standard

I Want to Teach My Child About Manners
 Printed in China.

Produced by Susan Lingo Books™
Cover and interior by Diana Walters

12 11 10 09 08 07 06 05 9 8 7 6 5 4 3 2 1
0-7847-1770-2

Contents

Introduction

Why teach your child about manners?

We live in a society full of hurried and harried schedules! It's wise to simplify as much as possible to keep our lives uncluttered, and manners training can be a significant help! Daily life becomes much more smooth and peaceful with the simple addition of phrases such as "I'm sorry," "please," and "thank you." And learning how to build relationships with caring courtesy at home will skyrocket our children to effectiveness in their walk with God, with friends at school, in bringing others to Jesus, and for future relationships and employment situations.

In the pages of *I Want to Teach My Child About Manners,* you'll help your child...

* Understand basic manners and politeness,
* Practice telephone etiquette,
* Develop table manners,
* Demonstrate family manners, classroom consideration, and respect for others,
* Learn manners for special occasions,
* Recognize the role manners play in honoring God—and more.

Families and cultures throughout the ages have made sets of rules to make life as orderly, peaceful, and enjoyable as possible for everyone. Your household manners may not look exactly the same as other families, but a basic set of personal and public politeness is essential for each of us. Take the time to evaluate and teach the manners that you know are important to your child, your family, and God. Your busy life will be simpler and more blessed because of it!

Jennie Bishop

Where Do You Stand?

Working toward helping your child learn about manners and how they affect his life is an important part of parenting. The following questionnaire will help you evaluate your own strengths and weaknesses and where your own values and philosophies fit in. Circle the number that best corresponds to your answer.

OPTIONS

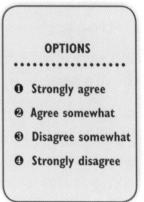

❶ Strongly agree
❷ Agree somewhat
❸ Disagree somewhat
❹ Strongly disagree

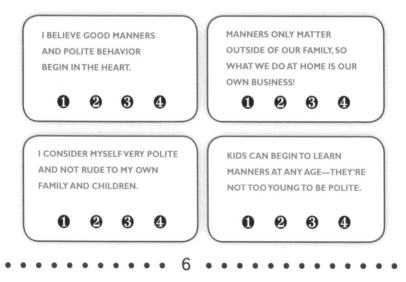

I BELIEVE GOOD MANNERS AND POLITE BEHAVIOR BEGIN IN THE HEART.

   ❹

MANNERS ONLY MATTER OUTSIDE OF OUR FAMILY, SO WHAT WE DO AT HOME IS OUR OWN BUSINESS!

I CONSIDER MYSELF VERY POLITE AND NOT RUDE TO MY OWN FAMILY AND CHILDREN.

KIDS CAN BEGIN TO LEARN MANNERS AT ANY AGE—THEY'RE NOT TOO YOUNG TO BE POLITE.

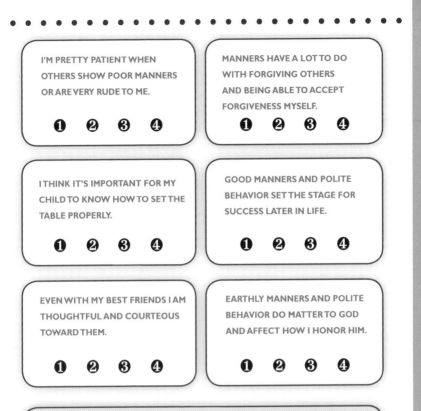

I'M PRETTY PATIENT WHEN OTHERS SHOW POOR MANNERS OR ARE VERY RUDE TO ME.

❶ ❷ ❸ ❹

MANNERS HAVE A LOT TO DO WITH FORGIVING OTHERS AND BEING ABLE TO ACCEPT FORGIVENESS MYSELF.

❶ ❷ ❸ ❹

I THINK IT'S IMPORTANT FOR MY CHILD TO KNOW HOW TO SET THE TABLE PROPERLY.

❶ ❷ ❸ ❹

GOOD MANNERS AND POLITE BEHAVIOR SET THE STAGE FOR SUCCESS LATER IN LIFE.

❶ ❷ ❸ ❹

EVEN WITH MY BEST FRIENDS I AM THOUGHTFUL AND COURTEOUS TOWARD THEM.

❶ ❷ ❸ ❹

EARTHLY MANNERS AND POLITE BEHAVIOR DO MATTER TO GOD AND AFFECT HOW I HONOR HIM.

❶ ❷ ❸ ❹

HOW YOU SCORED

16 or less Good manners are your friends! You realize that manners matter and that polite, compassionate behavior draws others to you, makes life more pleasant, and allows you to serve God and others more fully. Keep up the mannerly work!

17—24 Your manners may need a bit of polishing! Though you probably recognize the importance of good manners in public, you may be somewhat rude or demanding at home or with your friends. Politeness takes a bit of work and patience, but you can do it!

over 24 Your good manners may be hidden by a bit of self-centeredness. Remember that good manners and polite behavior draw others to us and are what Jesus modeled to others in His ministry. Polish your politeness and shine up your manners—you'll be surprised at the wonderful ways they affect your life and the lives of others close to you!

Manners Always Matter

Manners are a vital part of reflecting Christ to others. As we follow the rules of politeness for our culture and exhibit kind, thoughtful, unselfish behavior, we show people the genuine, sensitive love God has for them.

Manners are learned behaviors.

We don't emerge from the womb with the knowledge of good manners and etiquette (rats!). But we aren't born with *bad* manners, either. Accepted and gracious patterns of behavior must be learned. Our children need to watch those who model manners to learn how to behave with courtesy and caring. Our responsibility is to provide the best examples of "how Jesus would do it."

Manners are a system of how we speak and act.

Read Philippians 2:3, 4 and discuss what it means to be unselfish.

- *What do the phrases "selfish ambition" and "vain conceit" mean?*
- *If you "consider others better," does that mean you're no good?*
- *Who can you put first today?*

Through the ages, cultures and families have made rules of kindness, fairness, and grace to make life more enjoyable for everyone involved. However, in almost any circumstance, there is an accepted way of acting that keeps our interaction orderly and pleasant, with the other person's feelings and comfort in mind. Though these rules are not listed in the Bible, they are based on biblical concepts of putting others ahead of ourselves.

Children who grow up without training in manners and etiquette often feel uncomfortable in social settings and less confident in dealing with others. This way of life is based on Christ's clear teaching: We're to think of others ahead of ourselves, not putting ourselves down, but confidently and graciously lifting others up and seeing everyone as valuable in God's sight.

TIPS FOR TODDLERS

You can begin to teach your toddler manners by firmly saying, "No thank you" instead of just "no." Use "please" and "thank you" whenever possible with your toddlers.

If we trust God to do big things in our children and to empower them to change the world around them, we must accept the responsibility to train them in communicating confidently and in ways that reflect Jesus. A foundational knowledge of manners will enhance effectiveness in every facet of our children's lives—spiritually, morally, emotionally, physically, and relationally.

key point
MANNERS ARE RULES OF UNSELFISHNESS.

key point

MANNERS REFLECT JESUS' ATTITUDES.

To exhibit Christ and His love, respect rules that help us act in kind ways with deference toward others.

The discipline of manners may take a bit of time and effort at first, but it will pay off as unselfish communication and actions are adopted. Start with the basics of "please" and "thank you." At home or in public, whether you are passing food or picking up toys, encourage family members to ask, not order, with patience and grace. As manners become ingrained, your whole family will feel more comfortable, valued, and appreciated!

Manners are modeled by adults.

Don't be too hard on yourself—no parent is perfect. God gave your child to you because you are the right parent for her. In light of this, be aware that she will learn more behaviors from you than from any book or schoolteacher. Observing your manners affects how your child treats others. The way you react to a cashier, the driver ahead of you, or a waitress matters! Your words and actions are taken in, and eventually imitated, by the little one accompanying you.

PARENTS POINTER

Take a moment to pray if you are struggling with impatience and discourtesy toward your child. Many parents share the same guilt. Unhealthy drives to "do, do, do" make anyone short with others. Confess this to God and allow His Spirit to transform and renew your mind and heart—and perhaps your schedule!

Set powerful examples in practicing courtesy and good manners toward others.

Special reverence is good in a church setting, but kindness and courtesy should be practiced in-service or out. Beware of modeling double standards to your children! Often "church people" appear very polite at church but act selfishly to each other at home. Our walk with Christ is to be consistent, no matter the setting, or we will be viewed as less than genuine by believers and unbelievers alike.

key point
YOUR CHILD WATCHES YOUR EXAMPLES!
GOD HELPS US BECOME GOOD MODELS.

Set the standard for manners at home. Say, "please," "thank you," and "I'm sorry." Be quick to ask for forgiveness. Say "excuse me" if you bump into your child. Offer to help family members with chores. And remember: God strongly supports our desire to be more kind and loving toward others, for when we honor others with kind manners, we also honor God.

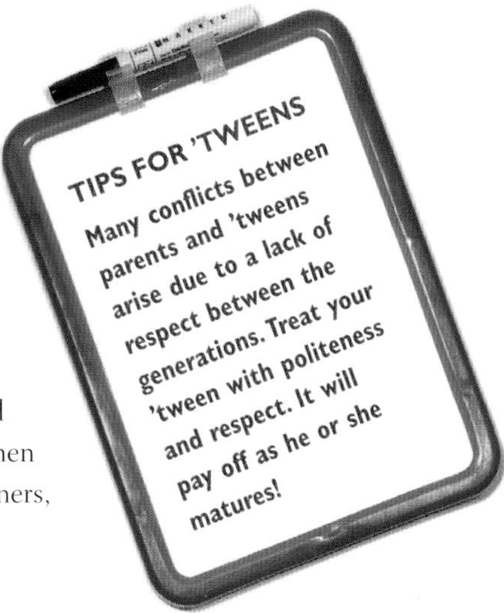

TIPS FOR 'TWEENS
Many conflicts between parents and 'tweens arise due to a lack of respect between the generations. Treat your 'tween with politeness and respect. It will pay off as he or she matures!

Remember:
The five most important words or phrases parents can use—and use often—are:

Please

Thank you

I'm sorry

Excuse me

I love you!

It is important for your child to know that he isn't just an obstacle in your path or an interruption in your plans. If your words and actions show that he is more important to you than your schedule, work, or television and that you can take time with him when he needs you, he will be much more able to grasp the concept of putting others first. When that relationship is a healthy priority, your life will be blessed as God planned, and manners can be put into practice quite naturally!

A LOVING RELATIONSHIP IS THE MOST BASIC TEACHING TOOL OF GOOD MANNERS!

Outward manners reflect inner attitudes.

Manners reflect our willingness to see others as more important than ourselves. As Christians, manners are a prerequisite to reflecting Christ. The good ways we treat others show we value them as Christ does.

Etiquette is "by the book."

TIPS FOR TODDLERS

Tea Time! Toddlers love tea parties, so invest in a child's tea set. Having a tea party with your little one is a great way to introduce and practice manners.

Every culture has sets of rules that govern what is "appropriate" in various circumstances. These are called rules of etiquette. You can visit your local library to find books by Emily Post, "Miss Manners," and others that give a comprehensive list of manners for a myriad of occasions. No one can master every rule perfectly, but a general understanding will make children more confident in their interactions with others.

Make etiquette fun—not a chore!

Even three-year-olds should be able to master a few simple rules of etiquette, such as looking into someone's eyes when they speak, saying "hello," washing hands before meals, and using silverware properly. Preschoolers can master staying seated to eat, taking turns, and saying "please" and "thank you."

key point
ETIQUETTE: RULES FOR CULTURAL PROPRIETY.

Find books about manners at your local library and share them with your child. Point out and praise the manners you often see and talk about new ones the family can practice together. Family time at meals is always a good time to teach manners, perhaps focusing on one rule of behavior each time the family enjoys a meal together. Little boys can be taught to let ladies go first, and little girls can help open doors for others.

Check out a manners book for your child from the library, then read it aloud with her as you discover new, exciting ways of being polite. (And don't forget, busy parent—you get to sit down and relax while you're sharing!)

Read Philippians 2:5-8 and discuss the kinds of attitudes Jesus modeled. Then ask your child the following questions:

- ***What is "the nature of a servant"?***
- ***How willing was Jesus to serve others?***
- ***How can we follow Jesus' example of serving others?***

Remind your child that taking on the nature of a servant is not always easy—but Jesus promised to help us by the power of His Spirit within us.

Most important, make etiquette fun and not a chore! Burdening your child with a list of "have-tos" and "must-nots" is counterproductive. Interact, laugh about your mistakes, and explore caring and communication as you nurture polite habits. The rules of etiquette are just one part of being polite—and rules without a warm relationship with your child will most often end in rebellion!

Manners are "by the heart."

Joining people in sorrow or happiness is a behavior Jesus taught by example. Read Romans 12:15 and discuss times when Jesus did this:

- **with Lazarus's sisters (John 11:32-36)**
- **at the wedding feast at Cana (John 2:1-11)**

Who is someone you can mourn or rejoice with today?

Dolls help children explore and develop tender, compassionate feelings.

Not all rules are written down. Sometimes just knowing the right thing to do comes out of a genuinely caring, loving heart and not from philosophical words about etiquette or manners. This ability can develop into a sharp sensitivity as we spend time knowing God and becoming like Him through His Word, prayer, and a lifestyle of worship and service. The tenderness we feel for others as the Holy Spirit increases our love leads us to wisdom in knowing when to talk or hold a hand, when to give a gift, or how to offer a kind act of servanthood.

God often helps us sense the right words to say or ways to help someone.

TIPS FOR 'TWEENS

In guiding your son to practice thoughtfulness, use the example of sports teams. There are rules they must follow, like the "by the book" manners we know are appropriate. But someone can follow the rules and still be rude. How does your son like to be treated when he's at practice or in the midst of a game? Ask for specifics and discuss how he can be polite and considerate, on and off the field.

Developing empathy is important. Affirm your child's natural compassion toward animals. A child who ministers to a bird with a broken wing will be more likely to understand and offer compassion toward a hurting person. Sympathize with your child if a family pet dies. People with a deeper belief in the value of all life are desperately needed in our world today. Encourage your child to think of others' needs first.

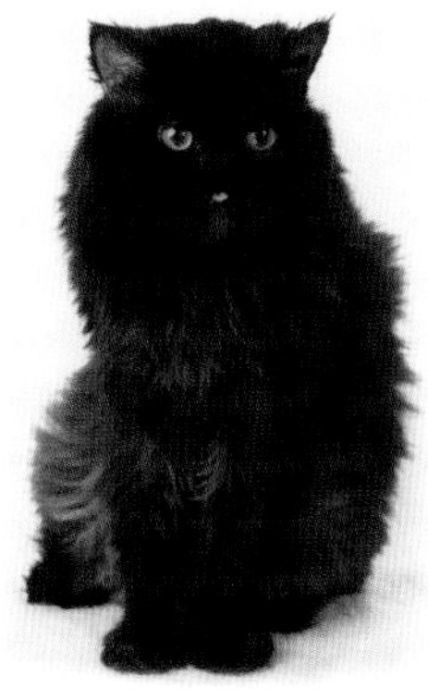

Jesus was tough and direct when He needed to be, but He also wept for others, reached out to those in need, and was patient and gentle with those who hurt. Our boys especially need to be validated in their feelings of gentleness to become loving husbands and fathers.

When a Pet Dies ...

A pet's death is a wonderful opportunity to talk about our own joyous "home-going."

DO ...

- Cry with your child, hug him, or just sit with him.
- Allow him to plan a simple burial ceremony.
- Help him recall happy memories with the pet.

DON'T ...

- Be afraid to answer tough questions with "I don't know."
- Rush a child through his emotions.
- Miss opportunities to share what heaven will be like.

Stories about Jesus are wonderful ways to teach your child about manners that come from the heart. Share how Jesus welcomed the little children, healed the sick, accepted Zacchaeus, and wept over Lazarus. As your child grows and gains wisdom, he will learn how to allow the Holy Spirit to move him with expressions of heartfelt compassion for others.

Manners affect our relationships.

The Bible says that "a gentle answer turns away wrath, but a harsh word stirs up anger" (Proverbs 15:1). Our manners (or lack thereof) have an impact on every relationship, whether we're speaking with Grandma, the boss, or a teacher.

Poor manners push others away.

Have you ever had someone walk into a doorway ahead of you and slam the door shut instead of holding it open for you? Lack of manners evokes feelings that the person offending is uncaring, cold, and to be avoided. Poor manners spread like a nasty disease, pushing people away from each other and separating us in a way that makes us unproductive and unhappy.

The root meaning for the word "sarcasm" is "to strip off flesh." Sounds like a dangerous way to communicate, doesn't it? Think twice before expressing yourself in this way in front of or to your kids—or anyone else!

key point
BAD MANNERS PUSH OTHERS AWAY.

Unkindness we experience in childhood is often so painful that we carry the memories throughout our lives. We may even put up walls that keep us from becoming the person God planned. Help your child see that encouragement makes people feel warm and affirms them as valuable. Manners play a big part in helping make the world a happy place with peaceful people!

key point
RUDENESS STARTS A VICIOUS CYCLE.

Harsh, rude, or thoughtless words make people angry. Read Proverbs 15:1, then discuss the following questions with your child.

- *What does "wrath" mean?*
- *What words can be used to "turn away wrath"?*
- *What happens when you "stir up" a swarm of bees?*

Then share a prayer with your child asking for God's help in controlling anger and showing kindness.

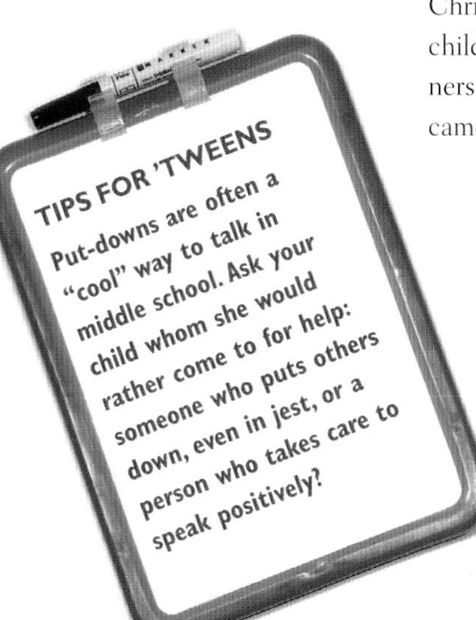

TIPS FOR 'TWEENS
Put-downs are often a "cool" way to talk in middle school. Ask your child whom she would rather come to for help: someone who puts others down, even in jest, or a person who takes care to speak positively?

It may seem unfair, but friends, teachers, family members, and coaches are more apt to avoid kids who do not show self-control and sensitivity. Children often feel unnecessary injustice because they have not been taught basic rules of manners and may see the world as unfair. The more this attitude grows, the more disagreeable these kids become to others.

Sarcasm, rude manners, and put-downs create a cycle of low morale that Jesus came to break. It's vital for your child to realize that people who refuse to express good manners and kind behavior are not the people others rely on or trust in. As Christians, we need to teach our children to use kindness and manners to reflect the love that Jesus came to give.

"Manners easily and rapidly mature into morals."
—Horace Mann

Good manners are like a people magnet.

Ask your child to pretend he's working in a fast-food restaurant where two people order food. One says, "May I have a hamburger, please?" and the other says, "Hamburger and fries, and hurry it up!" Which customer would your child rather serve and why? People with good manners tend to create an aura of peace that helps others relax and become open and friendly.

TARGET MOMENT

Remember: Your encouragement goes further than your correction. Take every opportunity to praise your child for heartfelt, good manners!

People are naturally attracted to kindness. Hosts beam when guests say "thank you" or bring a gift. Guests glow when they're welcomed into a home and treated politely. Hospitality is a wonderful ministry of good manners and genuine caring. We can make someone *feel at home* by treating him with warmth and as a "member of the family." And indeed, making someone feel welcomed into your family is welcoming them into God's family, too!

key point
GOOD MANNERS DRAW OTHERS CLOSE.

DON'T FORGET

How can your child make others feel like "part of the family"?

- Meet and greet them warmly: "I'm so glad to know (or see) you!"
- Pay a sincere compliment: "Your new dress is so beautiful."
- Extend an invitation: "Would you like to come, too?"
- Smile, smile, smile!

key point
KINDNESS MAKES OTHERS FEEL LIKE FAMILY.

Kids who write or draw cards for others usually have them posted on the recipient's refrigerator. A polite child is more likely to gain his teacher's or coach's attention. And that same child will certainly fare better with his boss and co-workers later in life. Many employees are hired because of their ability to work with people, and many of those employees keep their jobs longer for the same reason. Manners really *do* matter!

Make an extra effort to praise your child for specific instances when she makes herself a "magnet" today. Say something like, "I love it when you help someone feel happy!" or "I heard you say 'thank you' to Grandma when she gave you a cookie. That was very nice!" Be as delighted with your child as God is with us when we choose to obey Him.

Manners Are for Every Age

By age THREE:

- Establish eye contact when speaking.
- Say hello and greet friends.
- Wash hands before and after a meal.
- Stay seated during a meal.
- Use utensils at the table.
- Say "please" and "thank you."
- Help clean up messes or their rooms.
- Do a few simple chores at home.
- Pick up their clothes and toys.
- Chew with their mouths closed.

By age SIX:

- Set the table correctly.
- Clear the table after meals.
- Eat and drink slowly.
- Carry on conversations at the table.
- Offer to help around the house.
- Offer to help when visiting relatives.
- Make their beds.
- Take responsibility for a few regular chores.
- Answer the phone politely.
- Take a message on the phone.
- Introduce themselves to teachers or new friends.
- Write or draw simple tank-you notes.
- Say grace or a blessing before meals.

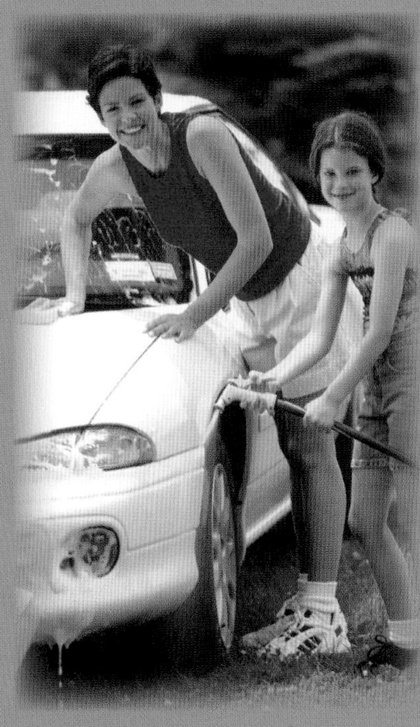

By age TEN:

- Be able to hold a conversation with an adult.
- Answer the telephone properly and take careful messages.
- Show self-control in public places.
- Demonstrate phone manners and take messages.
- Take responsibility for keeping the bedroom neat.
- Stand when an adult enters the room.
- Show control with voice levels.
- Show control with anger or frustration.
- Know how to be on time and plan accordingly.
- Take responsibility for their words and actions.
- Thank their host/hostess.

By age THIRTEEN:

- Initiate conversation and show interest with adults.
- Pick up after herself and her friends at home.
- Maintain a noise level that is acceptable to the family.
- Be protective and kind towards younger siblings.
- Express appreciation to parents and others.
- Write thank-you notes for gifts and special visits.
- Look for ways to help others without being asked.
- Hold doors open for others and show thoughtfulness.
- Do a job or chore cheerfully without expecting pay.
- Look for ways to willingly help or serve others.

How We Speak

God's Word makes it clear that we should speak only what builds others up (Ephesians 4:29). The key is choosing the right words in the right order for the right time, with sensitivity and some understanding of basic rules of courtesy, etiquette, and compassion.

Words are powerful first impressions.

We know that first impressions are important when it comes to appearances. Words clothe us as powerfully as fabric. It's important to choose our words wisely—especially our first words of welcome or greeting!

Greet others graciously.

key point
FIRST IMPRESSIONS DO COUNT!

Cheery greetings make smiles for both the giver and the receiver.

Have you noticed the greetings that open many New Testament epistles? The writers of these letters began with encouraging words such as, "Grace and peace to you from God our Father and the Lord Jesus Christ." They addressed the readers and listeners directly, blessed them, and prepared their hearts to receive the messages that were to follow. If this example was included so many times in the Holy Scriptures, it's likely that we should make an effort to do the same in our daily communications.

BIG
BIBLE
POINT

"I thank my God every time I remember you" (Philippians 1:3).

Explain to your child that many New Testament letters begin with special greetings. Read aloud the verse above, then discuss the following.

- **How does greeting someone make him feel special?**
- **How does greeting someone show respect?**
- **Who can you greet in a special way this week?**

Teach simple introductory greetings such as, "Hello. I'm Jennifer. It's nice to meet you." This will help your child overcome any lack of self-confidence. After the "ice is broken," the fun part of visiting can begin, and your child will feel more at ease. If your child shrinks back in fear, don't force her greeting. Avoid telling others your child is shy—self-fulfilling prophecies do happen! Encourage and equip your child with ways to acknowledge and greet others.

Children under three should be able to make eye contact and say "hello." By the age of five, a child should be able to give a more formal greeting, introduce herself, and address the adult by title and name, such as "Mr. Smith." Addressing others as "Sir" or "Ma'am" is always in gracious taste, and kids should always address adults using their titles unless otherwise told.

key point
CHEERFUL "HELLOS" OPEN HEARTS.

key point
GREETING OTHERS SHOWS RESPECT.

TRY THIS!

Role play with your child to help equip him with greetings for different situations and people. Have fun thinking of polite ways to say "hello" to people such as an aunt, a younger child, a teacher, or even the president!

Phones are like electronic handshakes.

If a phone call was a handshake, how would it feel? Like a handshake, our phone manners are part of the impressions we make on others. Not seeing the other person's face doesn't give us license to ignore courtesy. In fact, it's more important to use a pleasant voice when our faces are out of sight. Smiles can be "heard" over the phone even when they're not seen by the listener.

PARENTS POINTER

How young is too young for a cell phone? Here are considerations to keep in mind…

- **Will the phone be lost or misplaced?**
- **Will the phone be taken to school and become troublesome?**
- **Will your child opt for phone time instead of family time?**
- **Does you child know how to care for the phone?**
- **Can your child track his minutes of use?**

95 percent of those surveyed about phone safety were unaware of potential radiation hazards from cell phones. Remember: the smaller the phone, the more exposure to dangerous radiation!

TIPS FOR TODDLERS

Consider purchasing toy phones for you and your little one. Practice simple phone greetings such as "hello" or "good-bye" and hanging up the phone gently.

key point
USE A PLEASANT PHONE VOICE.

key point
RESPECT FAMILY TIME AND PRIVACY.

Kids love using and answering the telephone! And if a child is old enough to answer the phone, she's old enough to learn proper phone etiquette and manners. Teach your child a basic greeting such as, "Hello. This is John speaking," and have him politely ask, "Who is calling, please?" Explain the importance of using a pleasant phone voice when starting or ending a conversation.

It's important to teach your child not to give out certain information over the phone, including his full name or address. Show your child how to cover the receiver with his hand or lay it down gently when he's calling someone to the phone. Teach him how to say, "May I take a message, please?" and to write a simple phone message with a number and a name.

As your child grows and becomes more social, introduce rules that govern the appropriate lengths of phone conversations and respect for others' needs, including appropriate hours for calls (not during mealtimes or late in the evening). Remind your child that he can "wear out his welcome" with a phone call in the same way a person can overstay a visit.

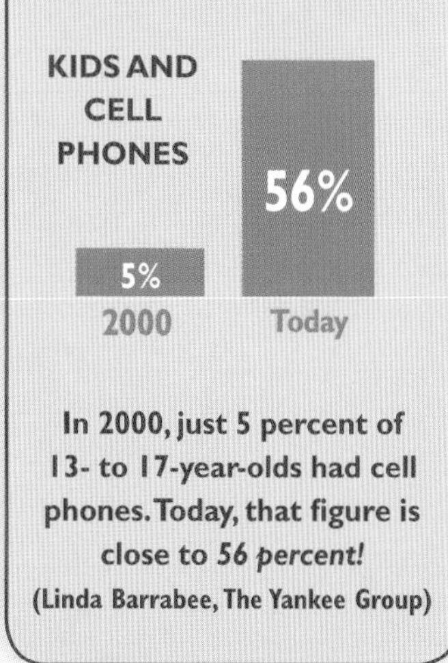
KIDS AND CELL PHONES
5%
56%
2000
Today

In 2000, just 5 percent of 13- to 17-year-olds had cell phones. Today, that figure is close to *56 percent!*
(Linda Barrabee, The Yankee Group)

Words are windows to the heart.

Words are like windows that allow the hearer to see right into our hearts. Positive words are powerful and can make the difference in someone's day!

Chats and spats are powerful communicators.

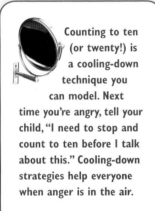

Counting to ten (or twenty!) is a cooling-down technique you can model. Next time you're angry, tell your child, "I need to stop and count to ten before I talk about this." Cooling-down strategies help everyone when anger is in the air.

Handling conflict is tricky, but it is possible to use restraint in diffusing difficult discussions. It's easy to say something we'll regret later, and even kids understand that the tongue is often quicker than the mind. Remind your child to think before she speaks—to breathe deeply, reflect, and maybe walk away to allow time to think about what to say … or *not* to say.

key point
CHOOSE YOUR WORDS CAREFULLY!
key point
WORDS CAN HEAL OR HURT.

The volume and tone of voice during a difficult conversation is important. Seek first to understand what has happened and examine the facts with phrases like, "Can you help me understand?" It's painful for everyone involved when someone places blame without even knowing what happened. Guide your child to question the action without being accusing.

BIG
BIBLE
POINT

"A word aptly spoken is like apples of gold in settings of silver," says Proverbs 25:11. Proverbs 15:1 also tells us that a gentle answer turns away wrath. Evaluate your communication during conflicts and how your choice of words affects the outcomes.

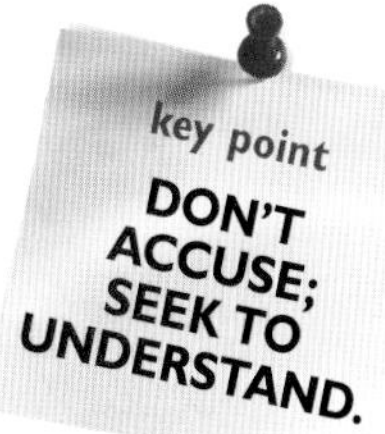
key point
DON'T ACCUSE; SEEK TO UNDERSTAND.

TARGET MOMENT

Ask your child what the saying "Think before you speak" means. Chat about why this is a wise saying and what can happen if we speak without thinking first.

Yelling and name-calling are contagious habits that easily spiral into unproductive accusations and hurt feelings. Instead of rolling your eyes, gasping in disbelief, or making unkind comments, sit down with the person you're in conflict with and give him your full attention. This is a God-given opportunity to overcome a problem together and grow closer. Remind your child that our words and actions speak volumes!

When the right words and attitudes are present, there is usually an opportunity to hug, touch gently, and pray together after a conflict. Often these actions will diffuse the disagreement entirely and resolve the situation at hand. If your child slips and calls someone a name or uses hurtful words, a sincere apology works wonders at restoring healthy communication—and happy hearts.

Encourage one another; build each other up.

Good manners include good listening skills.

Good listening is an important skill children need to learn. Because the world is still so new and exciting and there are so many wonderful things to share, kids have the tendency to chatter on rather than listen. Listening carefully and sincerely is an invaluable skill that demonstrates respect—and is a powerful, Christ-like gift you can offer to others!

TARGET MOMENT

If your child is constantly drawing attention to himself, consider that he may need more attention from you. Schedule time together and let him know you care and are listening!

We have two ears, two eyes, and one mouth—that means twice as much listening and looking as speaking!

Busy parents often have a tough time listening because of their hurried schedules. After a long day, we may not be excited about the dress our daughter's friend wore to school, but these things are the stuff of our kids' lives, and they want to share them even if the timing isn't perfect. If we ignore their attempts at conversation consistently, a day will come when our children will ignore us as well!

Kids enjoy playing "Grandma's Purse." Player one says, "I'm going to put in Grandma's purse ... an anteater." The second player repeats the phrase and adds an item. Continue repeating and adding new items.

key point
GOOD
MANNERS
KNOW WHEN
TO BE SILENT.

With a younger child, you'll need to guide the skills necessary for listening. Try playing a favorite song and ask your child to listen for a certain sound or instrument and clap each time he hears it. Explain that we need to take turns in both speaking and listening just as we take turns at games. If your child seems to interrupt a lot, a simple reminder that "It's Daddy's turn to talk right now" will reinforce the idea of speaking and listening in turns without interrupting.

Respectful communication includes good listening skills, but be careful to be a good listener yourself. It's impossible to nurture a relationship with a 'tween who is constantly lectured to but not listened to. Remember: rules without relationship often end in rebellion! The Bible clearly commands that we honor our parents, but it also states that fathers (and mothers) are not to exasperate their children (Ephesians 6:4).

*"We must be **silent** before we can **listen**. We must **listen** before we can **learn**. We must **learn** before we can **prepare**. We must **prepare** before we can **serve**. We must **serve** before we can **lead**."*
—William Arthur Ward

PARENTS POINTER

Improve listening skills by practicing "active listening." After you have listened to your child, respond by saying, "What I hear you saying is.... " This clarifies the communication, increases listening power, and avoids misunderstandings.

Rudeness hurts everyone.

The nature of God is love, and being rude does not reveal that love. No matter how busy we are, we must always make time to be polite—not just in words but in actions.

It's not just what you say, but how you say it.

How many times have you heard the right words but seen insincerity in someone's eyes or facial expressions that didn't match the words? Teach your child how to speak graciously, looking into a person's face and eyes and speaking sincerely. Polite words must be accompanied by a pleasant facial expression and a friendly tone of voice to be authentically kind.

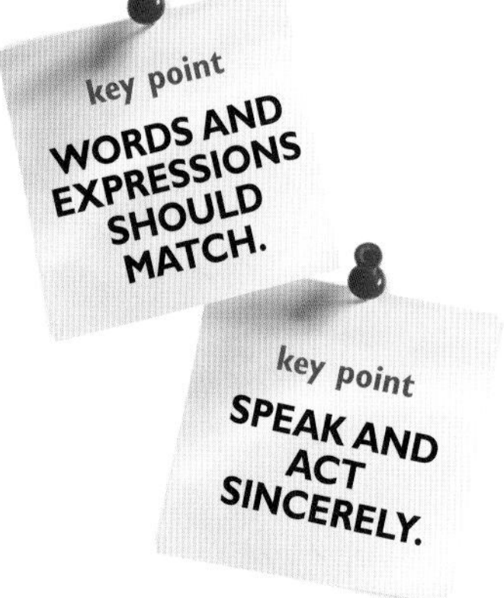

key point
WORDS AND EXPRESSIONS SHOULD MATCH.
key point
SPEAK AND ACT SINCERELY.

DON'T FORGET

Don't neglect the need to play with your children! Playing alleviates insecurities that often lead to rude or loud behavior arising from a lack of attention.

Explain that when words and expressions don't match, it's almost like telling a lie. Ask your child what the term "two-faced" means and why it's poor manners to speak one way and then act another. Insist on genuineness when "I'm sorry" must be said, both in heart and voice. Remind your child that good manners and honorable words must be followed with sincere expressions.

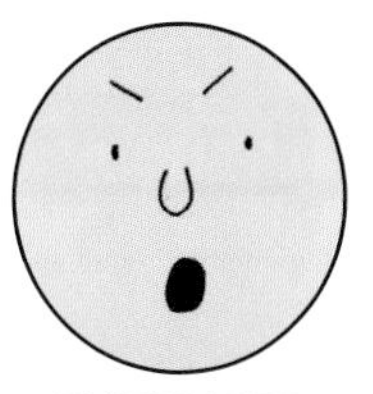

Preschoolers can identify facial expressions and words that match. Draw these faces on paper plates, then hold them up one by one. Make up a sentence to go with each face, such as "I feel happy." Try holding up a happy face and saying, "I feel mad!" Have your child say "yes" if your words match or "no" if they don't.

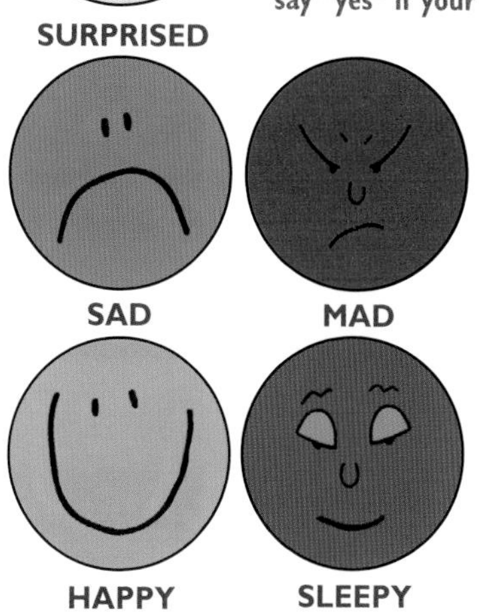

Write phrases such as "I don't like spinach" on copy paper. Take turns repeating the phrases in different ways, such as with sarcasm, excitement, or apathy. How do they take on different meanings with various intonations and facial expressions?

Whispering is one of the most used and abused forms of speaking among children. If it's an urgent situation where someone might be saved embarrassment, speak with the affected party in another room or speak very quietly. Whispering always sets up a "them" and "us" environment where everyone wonders if he is the one being discussed. Remind your child that our goal as Christians is to create a welcoming atmosphere that is polite, open, and inclusive where everyone feels valued, built up, and encouraged.

Do you often wish each of your children had a volume-control knob? Help your child learn appropriate levels of speech by stressing the difference between "indoor voices" and "outdoor voices." Ask politely for "indoor voices" when volume gets out of control. Yelling affects everyone in the house—even the family pet. Use normal speaking voices in public, but provide opportunities to be loud during playtime outside—that's just part of being a kid!

Taming the tongue is crucial.

God's Word teaches us that the tongue is a "restless evil, full of deadly poison" (James 3:8). Our words can be used to encourage and support or to cause hurt and trouble. Each person must "tame" his tongue and use words in positive ways. With children, matters of disrespect and unkind words must be immediately addressed to guide them away from using the tongue as a weapon instead as a tool to express love.

TRY THIS!

Purchase sour candies and sweet ones (or you can use lemon juice and sugar). Have your child hold out his tongue and place a sour taste on it. Ask your child to describe the flavor and what kinds of words might taste "sour." Then repeat this activity using a sweet taste. Remind your child that words can be sweet and good or sour and hurtful, so we must be careful to use words that are uplifting, good, and positive!

TARGET MOMENT

Sticks and stones may break my bones, but words can never hurt me. **A familiar childhood chant, but is it true? Can words hurt others? Discuss this rhyme with your child and why words can and do have the power to hurt!**

key point
OUR WORDS REQUIRE SELF-CONTROL.

Your child needs to have clear boundaries set for what kinds of words will not be tolerated. Make it clear there will be a price for unkind and disrespectful words, whether it is time in a quiet corner or extra chores. Speaking with acceptable words and kind expressions is valuable preparation for building relationships tomorrow and for deepening relationships with friends today.

Help your child realize that swearing is not the only negative way in which words might be used. Discuss hurt that is caused by name-calling and review the repercussions of cursing and using the Lord's name in vain. Define the difference between self-confidence and bragging and remind your child that gossiping can hurt others and may pass on things that are not true.

Top 6 reasons kids give for swearing or cussing:

1. **Because they're upset, frustrated, or hurt.**
2. **To show off for their friends.**
3. **To upset others or get attention.**
4. **To feel grown-up or "cool."**
5. **Because their family says the words.**
6. **They don't think swearing is rude.**

God devoted two commandments to the matter of speech. Read aloud Exodus 20:7, 16. Then discuss the following:

- *What does "taking the Lord's name in vain" mean?*
- *What does it mean to "bear false witness" against someone?*
- *Why do you think God wants us to tame our tongues?*
- *How can choosing and using our words carefully show obedience to God? respect for others?*

Encourage your child to ask forgiveness when he slips and uses unkind, angry, or hurtful words. If "no man can tame the tongue," as James 3:8 teaches, then we are all far from perfect—parent or child. Seeing our willingness humbly to ask forgiveness will encourage our children to deal honestly with their own slips of speech. And modeling the positive use of words to ask forgiveness sincerely is what taming the tongue is all about!

Speech that's polite can delight!

Do you have friends who are a breath of fresh air whenever you meet? That impression is often made by people who are in the habit of using words politely as they voice genuine concern for their listeners.

Express your gratitude.

key point
EXPRESSING THANKS EXPRESSES LOVE.
key point
LOOK FOR REASONS TO GIVE THANKS!

Showing gratitude builds up relationships. When we don't take the time to express thanks, we miss great opportunities to show Christ's love and express our own attitudes of gratitude. Children easily catch on to the concept of giving thanks, and most enjoy writing and decorating thank-you cards or making special trips or phone calls to say "thank you."

Help your child develop an awareness of the blessings around him. Point out a sunset or flower and say, "Thank You, God, for this beauty." Encourage your child to do the same. Pray together with thanks, not just with requests. From giving thanks at home, your child can move on to extending polite thanks to their friends' moms after sharing meals or an overnight stay.

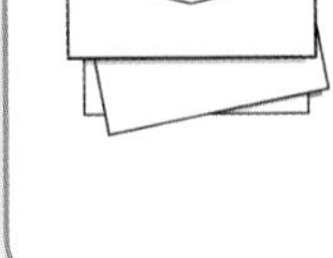

Remind your older child of the five basic parts of a thank-you note:

1. **Thank the giver.**
2. **Name the gift.**
3. **Share what you enjoy about the gift.**
4. **Choose a warm closing.**
5. **Sign your name.**

Kids love creating ways to express their thanks! From cards and calls to fresh-baked cookies, kids enjoy expressing thanks to family members and friends. Remind your child that thank-you notes are proper after receiving gifts, staying at someone's house overnight or while on vacation, and other acts of kindness. E-mail or phone thank-yous are convenient, but handwritten notes express thanks that can be read and enjoyed again and again!

Involve your child in creative expressions of gratitude and caring such as baking simple treats or painting a special thank-you.

Try making thank-you cards into a fun craft project to really involve your child! Provide construction paper and make stamps, stickers, and markers available. Craft stores often have precut and folded notepaper and envelopes ready to be embellished. When a child is younger, just signing her name or adding a simple drawing is sufficient and charming.

PARENTS POINTER

Use a simple table prayer of thanks to end meals and encourage your family to "stop and smell the roses." Let each person thank God for two things, then ask Mom or Dad to close.

Express your love.

Everyday expressions of love are vital to our health. Challenge your child to give a loving hug or say "I love you" to each family member at least three times a day. Simply tucking a loving note in your child's lunchbox or backpack can brighten his whole day. Pass the love on by helping your child tuck a loving note in Daddy's lunch—it will make his day, too. And one day you'll very likely find that your child is writing similar notes to you!

Do you regularly make time for simple, loving verbal expressions of kindness and affirm the words and expressions that your children offer to you? A simple "I'm glad you love me" expresses your love and also provides a model for your child's expressions. Many of us are unaware of our deep need for love and actually discount such outward expressions, but love is precisely what Jesus came to give!

TIPS FOR 'TWEENS

Read these verses to discover what Scripture says about loving a wide range of people—including God!

- *enemies or bullies (Matthew 5:44, 45)*
- *your neighbor (Matthew 19:19; 22:39)*
- *God (Matthew 22:37)*
- *your friend (Proverbs 17:17)*
- *strangers and others (1 John 4:21)*

Simply saying the words "I love you" is only one way to communicate love and compassion for family and others. Help your child explore different avenues of expression. Paint or draw a special picture to express love. Present flowers to someone or do a chore for a tired sibling or parent. Older kids may enjoy writing poems and then recording them to give to Grandma and Grandpa.

Read 1 John 4:7, 8 and discuss why loving others is key to a loving relationship with God.

- *Why do we need love?*
- *Where does love come from?*
- *Do our "love tanks" ever become empty when we love God? Explain.*
- *In what ways does love help us draw closer to God? to others?*

key point
WORDS ARE
NICE—
ACTIONS ARE
BETTER!

SIGNS OF LOVE! Teach your child how to use his hands, as well as his heart, to sign the words for "I love you" using American Sign Language! Check out www.aslinfo.com.

Help your child *live* the love he feels and remind him that we love because God first loved us (1 John 4:19), and we can spread God's love to others. Read aloud 1 Corinthians 13:4-8 and discuss what love is and how it is expressed. Then challenge your child to name three ways he can show his love this week. Encourage him to follow through and express himself!

key point
EVERYONE NEEDS LOVE!

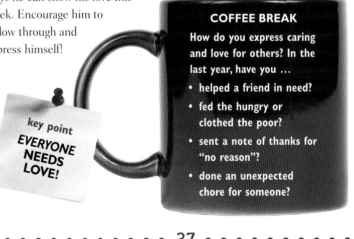

COFFEE BREAK

How do you express caring and love for others? In the last year, have you ...

- **helped a friend in need?**
- **fed the hungry or clothed the poor?**
- **sent a note of thanks for "no reason"?**
- **done an unexpected chore for someone?**

Our words to others speak volumes.

Wisely chosen words are crucial to the goal of showing good manners, encouraging others, and sharing Jesus. Simple, authentic, caring expressions are best—and last the longest!

Uplifting words are the best encouragement.

Think about a time you were at a loss for words or how to express your concern. These awkward moments can leave us wondering what good manners dictate should be said. Speaking kind, compassionate words of encouragement are often the best for these situations. Phrases such as "I know you can do it" or "I'm here for you" are often like rays of sunshine to another's heart.

Children can be taught that simple, genuine phrases such as "I care about you" show genuine concern that is welcome and healing. In the event of a funeral or a terminal illness, talk openly with your child about sharing good memories and giving encouragement with statements such as "I know God is here" and "I will pray for you."

PARENTS POINTER

Children love to help others with the natural sunshine they exude! What a perfect way to reach others with love. Help your child discover his spiritual potential by challenging him to start a "ministry of encouragement" whereby he passes on a smile, hug, or cheery card to one person a day!

key point
ENCOURAGING WORDS ARE LIKE SUNSHINE!

Ask your toddler what "happy words" she can say to make others smile. Remind her that words can be like a hug.

Take your child with you on compassionate visits whenever you can. Just the cheerful presence, chattiness, and brief attention of a child can be extremely soothing and encouraging to others, and your child's expressions of concern provide powerful reinforcement for the value of compassionate words.

key point
POSITIVE WORDS CHANGE ATTITUDES.

TIPS FOR 'TWEENS

Kids in middle school tend to focus on themselves. Help your 'tween focus on others' needs through food drives, get-well cards, or donations of clothing.

Don't forget that uplifting words aren't just for outreach occasions. Make a card for Dad or a sibling when he has had a hard day. Steer clear of speaking words of complaint or judgment and look for positive comments or compliments. Remind your child that he'll never know whose day might brighten because of a few encouraging words he took the time—and heart—to say!

TRY THIS!

Challenge your family to memorize Philippians 2:14, 15 and 1 Thessalonians 5:11. (Younger children can work on Philippians 2:14.) Write the words on paper and hang them up. Repeat the verses before meals and remind everyone that complaining does no one any good but encouraging words can change lives!

Prayerful words are the best help.

"Be joyful always; pray continually; give thanks in all circumstances" (1 Thessalonians 5:16-18). What beautiful verses that remind us of the power of our words before God! Help your child realize that there is power in sincere and constant prayer. By praying with you, your child will see your heart open before God and ready to receive all God offers us.

Assure your child that God is with him and listening to his prayers—and that even Jesus talked to God and taught the disciples how to pray. Take every opportunity to make your child aware of God's presence, not only through prayer, but by pointing out blessings and acts of obedience and forgiveness. Encourage your child to thank God openly as often as possible.

key point
PRAYER
IS
POWERFUL.

TRY THIS!

Decorate a family prayer box. Talk about prayers being treasured by God, then let the family place written prayers in the box. Don't forget to take them out as prayers are answered—and share the good news with your family!

key point
PRAYER
CONNECTS
US WITH
GOD.

key point
GOD HEARS AND ANSWERS PRAYERS.

Many children pray for others at a very young age, and their intercessions are a joy. Explain that God will help them know what to say as they ask for His leading. Stress that there is no wrong way to pray, as long as we love God and believe that He hears us. God understands a reverent "Dear God" and "amen" just as well as He understands "Help!"

BIG BIBLE POINT

Read Revelation 8:3, 4. Burn incense as you pray and watch it rise for a memorable prayer time.

- *Why did God choose to compare our prayers to incense?*
- *What kinds of words does God want us to use in our prayers?*
- *What does God desire even more than special words?*

Help your child to include four important elements in his prayers: "I love you" (adoration), "I'm sorry" (confession), "please, God" (supplication), and "thank you" (thanksgiving). And don't forget to teach your child to listen and wait for God's response! Set a time each day for your child to spend time chatting with God!

TIPS FOR TODDLERS

- **Make a special prayer mat to sit on during prayer time. Use markers to decorate a square of craft felt or a white towel to sit on.**
- **Let your child dictate his prayers. Write down a simple prayer as your child dictates to you. Tape it to a helium balloon and release it outside. Assure your child that prayers rise to God's ears—and His heart!**

Words have the power to worship God and witness to others!

key point
WORSHIP HONORS GOD.

key point
WORSHIP CHANGES LIVES!

Worship is much more than the music we sing on Sunday—it is an attitude of actions and words that we express every day, all day long! When others see us using words in this way, they learn what God is like and they want to know Him, too. Encouragement and evangelism naturally begin to take place.

FAMILY WORSHIP SERVICE

PLAN A FAMILY WORSHIP SERVICE BY ASSIGNING EACH PERSON IN THE FAMILY SOME PORTION OF YOUR SHARED WORSHIP EXPERIENCE.

- **Candle lighter** (light a candle)
- **Scripture reader** (choose and read a verse or two)
- **Opening prayer leader** (lead opening prayer)
- **Bible-story reader** (read portion of Bible story)
- **Song leader** (lead two songs)
- **Closing prayer leader** (lead closing prayer)
- **Candle blower** (blow out the candle)

Children can have incredible impact as witnesses. When we tell others about Jesus and what He's done in our lives, it's called being a "witness." Help your child write down his own witness in a few sentences. It will help him find the words to say to when he's ready to tell someone about Jesus.

- Sing worship songs.
- Tell God what you love about Him.
- Paint prayers to God.
- Learn a new Scripture verse.
- Act out a verse praising God.
- Have family communion.
- Draw pictures thanking God.
- Write poems praising God.

"Prayer does not change God, but it changes him who prays."
—Søren Kierkegaard

If your child has a question about a friend's or relative's standing in Christ, explain that questions about beliefs are best asked in private so the person doesn't feel put on the spot. Your child doesn't have to lead prayers or find fancy words telling about Jesus—just her question is a seed planted that God will use. Later, share a prayer for this friend and thank God for the encouraging words your child planted!

Words used to give God honor and to tell others about His greatness are the most powerful tools on earth. As you see your child use words that honor God, praise your child—and the Lord! Daily use of the simple phrase "Thank You, God" is always appropriate when it is spoken with a genuine, worshipful attitude.

WHAT GOOD MANNERS SAY!

Use this helpful chart to give you a good idea of what general speaking and communication manners kids need to nurture.

GREETINGS & CONVERSATION

- Make eye contact and smile.
- Greet others with "Hello" or "It's nice to see you."
- Don't interrupt—wait your turn to talk.
- Address adults by Mr., Mrs., Ma'am, or Sir unless otherwise told.
- Use conversation starters such as "How have you been?" "What have you been up to?" "How is everyone in your family?"
- Don't talk too loudly or too much.
- Close conversations with "It's been nice chatting with you" or "I hope to see you soon."
- Smile and say "good-bye."

PHONE MANNERS

- Answer politely by saying, "Hello, this is (*your name*)," "Good day, this is (*your name*)," or "(*Your name*) speaking, may I help you?"
- Offer to take a message if needed—then write it down.
- Don't give out personal information or your address.
- Cover the mouthpiece when calling someone to the phone.
- Thank the caller for calling.
- End your call with "Good-bye" or "Thank you for calling."
- Hang up the phone nicely.

THANK-YOUS & E-MAIL

- Write personal notes for gifts, special visits, or to thank a hostess for a nice time.
- Address the person by name in your note.

- Don't make your notes too general—make them specific.
- Mention the gift or reason for your thank-you note.
- Explain why you enjoy the gift or enjoyed your visit.
- Close you note with "Thank you again," "Sincerely," or "Your friend."
- Sign your note.
- Avoid using e-mail for thank-you notes—use it for "just thinking of you" notes.

ENCOURAGING WORDS

- Speak nicely to others.
- Use words that uplift or encourage others.
- Don't call others names.
- Don't gossip about others.
- Try some of these encouraging words or phrases: "You always make me smile" or "I'm always here to listen."
- Be sure your words match your actions. If you say you will help, then be sure to help!
- Be sincere in what you say.
- Avoid complaining—look on the bright side of problems.
- Remember to communicate through your actions; a smile or hug says "I love you" too!

SHARE YOUR WITNESS

- Tell others about Jesus and what He has done for you.
- Don't force others who are not willing to hear about Jesus. God will get them ready!
- Model kindness and compassion as Jesus did for others.
- Share what Jesus' love, forgiveness, and salvation mean.
- Open a conversation about Jesus by saying things such as, "Do you know that Jesus is our very best friend?" or "Isn't it great that Jesus loves us?"
- Share something that faith or prayer has done in your life.
- Pray for the people you witness to.

How We Behave

Words are just a part of good manners. Our polite words must be paired with mannerly, sincere, and loving actions for our lives to reflect Christ as they should.

Actions speak louder than words.

Our actions tell on us. There are no magic words that can speak louder than our behaviors. If a person says "Good morning," his tone and body language will show whether or not he *really* thinks that the morning is good. It's important for children to learn that words and actions must match and be sincere.

Manners communicate upbringing.

Families and their manners and habits follow along a continuum from very informal all of the time to very strict and formal. But one thing most families have in common is the desire to teach their children manners, polite behavior, and respectful attitudes. As you teach polite behavior for many circumstances, your child will be more self-confident and comfortable.

PARENTS POINTER

How do your habits reflect your own upbringing? Are there habits and behaviors you'd like to improve upon? Now is the time to make those changes! In doing so you improve yourself avoid passing along behaviors that may need changing later!

BIG
BIBLE
POINT

Read Proverbs 12:1 and 25:28. Consider why the exhausting task of growing disciplined, well-mannered children is well worth our efforts.

- *How do these verses relate to teaching manners?*
- *How can these verses encourage you to be consistent in good parenting habits?*

Mirror, mirror, on the wall—
Family manners are reflected to all!

Young people who are considerate of others are often rewarded with responsibilities and privileges. Their attention to others' needs and their polite behavior gain favor for them in the eyes of adults as well as peers. Showing kindness, deference, sensitivity, and consideration of others makes us nicer to be around!

Good habits of behavior prepare our children for life ahead. Your child will make his share of poor choices as he learns, but an overall understanding and practice of polite actions will benefit him for the rest of his life!

Patterns of upbringing aren't easy to change. With God's Spirit, and our determination to require good, loving, caring behavior from our children, we can prepare them to succeed no matter what our past upbringings may have been.

TIPS FOR 'TWEENS

Challenge your older child to hold a mirror up so it points across the room, then draw what he sees in the mirror. When the drawing is done, ask:

- *Why was this drawing activity a bit tricky?*
- *Did you draw exactly what you saw? Explain.*
- *How does a reflection mimic what is real?*
- *In what ways is this activity like reflecting to others the manners we use at home?*

key point
KIND BEHAVIOR MIMICS GOOD MANNERS.

key point
GOOD MANNERS BEGIN AT HOME!

Behavior communicates respect.

Respect, or a lack thereof, is communicated not only through our words but through our actions and attitudes as well. To respect others is to treat them in a way that shows they are valued. The practice of standing when an adult enters the room has gone out of fashion, but if your children do it a few times you will recognize how valued it makes an adult feel. Respect always improves self-worth—for both the giver and receiver!

key point
RESPECT TELLS OTHERS YOU VALUE THEM.

To impart a sense of respect in your child, you must first respect him by listening sincerely, valuing his thoughts, and treating him as you would Jesus. When you set examples that show respect, dignity, and sincerity, mutual respect develops. Jesus taught us to treat others as we wish to be treated. If we desire our kids to show respect, we must begin by respecting them!

key point
GIVE RESPECT TO GET RESPECT!

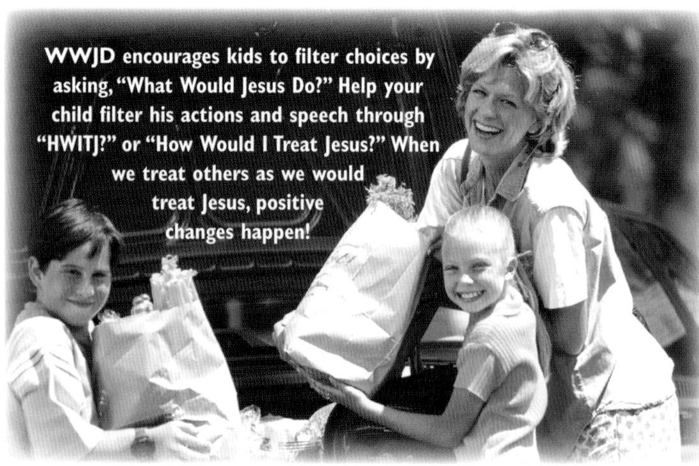

WWJD encourages kids to filter choices by asking, "What Would Jesus Do?" Help your child filter his actions and speech through "HWITJ?" or "How Would I Treat Jesus?" When we treat others as we would treat Jesus, positive changes happen!

Outward demonstrations of respect include actions as simple as facing someone when speaking to him or listening to what someone has to say without interrupting. Respect is also demonstrated through sharing. If your child learns to share her toys graciously, she will be more apt to share friends, conversation, and attention. Respect is shown through greeting others, holding doors open, and helping carry packages.

Remind your child that how we treat others and what we do for them, we also do for Jesus. It's only when we show genuine respect for others that we can give honest honor, respect, and reverence to God! Disrespectful and thoughtless attitudes demonstrate a selfishness that is counterintuitive to following Christ—and counterproductive to being a polite part of society!

BASIC ACTIONS OF RESPECT

- Look at others when they speak.
- Acknowledge others who enter a room.
- Put others' needs before yours.
- Take turns when speaking.
- Open doors for others.
- Listen attentively.

- Serve others first.
- Sit quietly after meals.
- Give others the "first" turn.
- Offer to help.
- Cover your mouth when you cough or sneeze.
- Say "Excuse me" or "Pardon me" as needed.

Show good manners at home.

Children who are required to behave considerately in the home will carry this behavior into public settings both now and later in their lives. It's worth it to make manners a priority at home!

Mealtime manners are the first course.

key point
MEALTIMES ARE TOGETHER TIMES!

Mealtimes at the table, with the media turned off, are key times for family members to share the happenings of the day and to stay emotionally connected to each other. Sit-down meals are also the main way a child picks up mealtime manners and etiquette. Everyone needs to know the basics of mannerly eating that make a meal pleasant for the whole family.

Allow your child to learn basic table settings: forks to the left of the plates, knives to the right, spoons next to the knives on the far right, and drinking glasses at the top right of dinner plates. Napkins can be folded under the forks or even folded neatly on dinner plates. Explain that, no matter how many utensils appear in a setting, the ones farthest from the plate will be used first.

TRY THIS!

Make a special place-setting placemat for your child. Draw a place setting on a sheet of construction paper and cover it with clear adhesive-backed plastic.

Studies show that well-adjusted children share the practice of eating with their families. Don't underestimate mealtime!

Show your child how to place the napkin on his lap when he sits down. Encourage him to take small bites, chew with his mouth closed, and always say "please" and "thank you." Embarrassing situations like burps or spills can be handled with a simple "Excuse me" or "I'm sorry."

key point
INSIST ON TABLE MANNERS!

Kids enjoy setting the table when they know where everything goes. Challenge your child to create new ways of folding the napkins!

Each family may make individual choices about what habits are important to them at mealtime, but all manners and habits should work together toward helping everyone enjoy the food and the company. After meals, leave napkins on the table and scoot chairs in. Teach your child to thank whoever prepared the meal and willingly offer to help clean up!

"MANNERS ARE A SENSITIVE AWARENESS OF THE FEELINGS OF OTHERS. IF YOU HAVE THAT AWARENESS, YOU HAVE GOOD MANNERS, NO MATTER WHAT FORK YOU USE."

—EMILY POST

Spread good manners around the house.

Every day holds a wealth of opportunities for teaching and learning manners that serve our families and friends. Learning to put others first develops a habit of service that sets Christian families apart. Each day you and your child can look for ways to inject manners and unselfish behavior into your family as you draw closer to one another and God.

Encourage your child to approach daily chores with a willing attitude that places others before him and encourages family teamwork. Explain that when we seek to serve one another, we also serve God. Thank your child for helping with the housekeeping and remind him that many hands make the work light—and the manners flow!

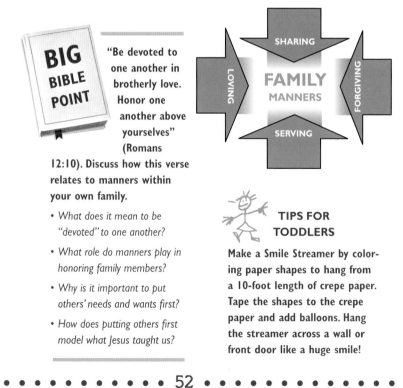

"Be devoted to one another in brotherly love. Honor one another above yourselves" (Romans 12:10). Discuss how this verse relates to manners within your own family.

- *What does it mean to be "devoted" to one another?*
- *What role do manners play in honoring family members?*
- *Why is it important to put others' needs and wants first?*
- *How does putting others first model what Jesus taught us?*

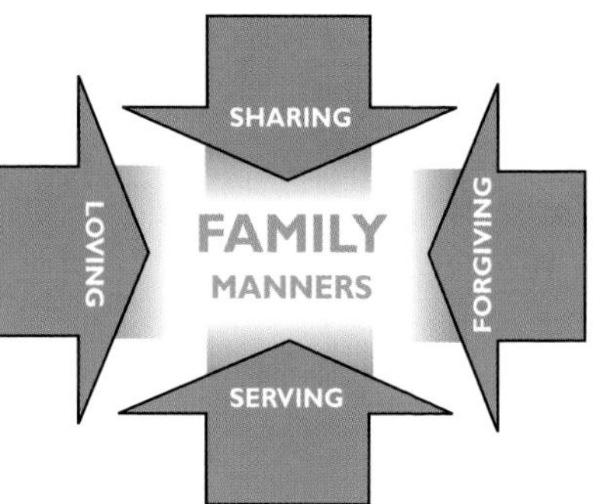

TIPS FOR TODDLERS

Make a Smile Streamer by coloring paper shapes to hang from a 10-foot length of crepe paper. Tape the shapes to the crepe paper and add balloons. Hang the streamer across a wall or front door like a huge smile!

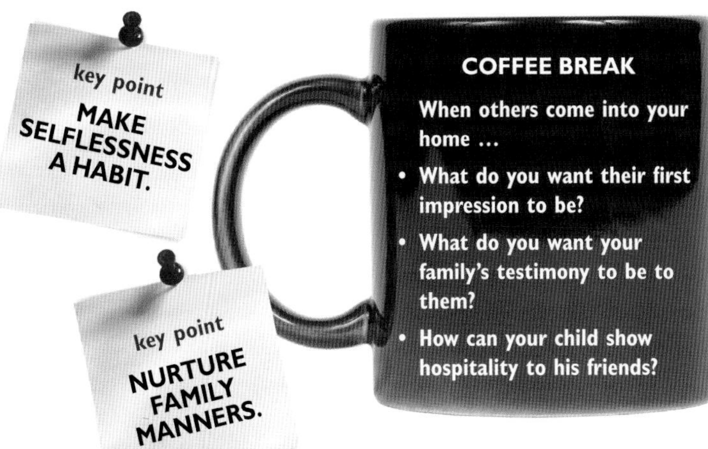

key point
MAKE SELFLESSNESS A HABIT.
key point
NURTURE FAMILY MANNERS.
COFFEE BREAK
When others come into your home ...
• What do you want their first impression to be?
• What do you want your family's testimony to be to them?
• How can your child show hospitality to his friends?

TRY THIS!

Express random acts of kindness through "Do, Make, Say, Bake" activities. Your child can *do* something kind for another family member (a chore) or *make* something (a card or picture to hang). Have your child *say* encouraging words and "*bake*" a treat for someone (cookies or jelly on crackers).

Hospitality toward guests is another way to practice manners at home. Greet guests and help with coats or bags. When your child has a friend spend the night, look for creative ideas to make her friend feel special and welcomed. Point out that when we graciously open our home to others, we're opening our hearts to them as well!

Brainstorm with your family different ways you can show RAKs (random acts of kindness) to one another. Write the ideas on slips of paper and place them in a jar. Take turns each week pulling out secret ideas to show your family compassion. Help make loving one another and showing politeness your most basic family goal by being courteous and kind every day.

Show good manners in public.

The more kids understand about being considerate and thoughtful of others, the more they embrace manners and etiquette—and become more confident in all public and formal occasions.

Manners count when eating out!

One of the most important demonstrations of good "manners" while eating out involves patience! While you wait for food to be served, encourage pleasant conversation, take turns in the bathroom, and prohibit the use of condiments for "entertainment." Bring paper on which to draw or chat about the events of the day and enjoy each other without disturbing others eating nearby.

TIPS FOR
TODDLERS

Scope out family eateries with coloring pages and children's menus. Don't choose just for junior, but be aware that meals may be more peaceful if the restaurant is geared for families.

key point
BE CONSIDERATE OF OTHER DINERS.

In a fast-food restaurant, certain special manners are required. Remind your child to step back from the counter until he knows what to order. Teach your child to take only the condiments, straws, and napkins he needs during his visit. Make it a point to leave your table (and floor area) picked up as a courtesy to the next diners.

key point
BE POLITE TO FOOD SERVERS.

Teach boys to remove their hats and pull chairs out for the ladies (not a bad habit in any restaurant). Be patient in teaching the use of new utensils and dishes and remind your child to leave her napkin on the chair if she is temporarily gone from the table—or beside her plate if she is done eating.

Sharing mealtime prayers show that we are genuinely grateful and prohibits a rude rush to inhale our food. If a waitress brings your food while you are praying, keep your prayer brief, but don't feel obligated to stop in mid prayer. Most waitresses will be patient and sensitive enough to hold the food until you are finished.

- **53% describe dinner as a sit-down family event.**
- **59% say dining as a family is very important.**
- **73% of families eat out at least twice a month.**
- **58% say they're too busy to cook.**

BIG BIBLE POINT

Saying "grace" is a powerful way of showing respect and for God and His provision. Read aloud I Thessalonians 5:18 and discuss why giving thanks before meals honors God and shows good manners.

key point
RESTAURANT MANNERS AFFECT EVERYONE.

Manners matter during formal occasions.

Showing consideration for others in the case of parties, weddings, and especially funerals is essential. Your child will need preparation and guidance to behave appropriately and sensitively. These functions are not only wonderful opportunities to learn more about manners but are important milestone events that prepare children for the coming passages of their own lives.

TARGET MOMENT

When your child attends his first funeral, be especially sensitive to what God may be teaching him during these events that focus on the clear connection between physical and spiritual life.

At funerals, the most appropriate words a child can offer are, "I'm sorry for your loss." Compassion speaks far more than words in tender situations, so encourage your child to listen more and speak less. Clearly explain what will happen at the funeral or wake and answer as many questions as possible beforehand. Make it clear that no running or horseplay will be allowed.

key point
MILESTONE EVENTS TEACH KIDS ABOUT LIFE.
key point
SPECIAL OCCASIONS REQUIRE SENSITIVITY.
For special occasions with your toddler, provide a few items to pass the time quietly:
• small pretzels or crackers
• a small toy with moving parts
• a small puzzle
• crayons and a coloring book

SPECIAL TIMES REQUIRE SPECIAL MANNERS!

Children (especially little girls) look forward to weddings, but sometimes young children think these wonderful parties are for them instead of the brides and grooms! Be sure to stress the fact that this day is to honor and celebrate the marriage of the bride and groom. Encourage your child to stand when the bride enters, to congratulate the couple after the service with handshakes and smiles, and to be respectful, quiet, and attentive during the service. Review how to make polite introductions, since your child may be meeting a number of new people. If your child is part of the wedding party, don't allow her to "steal the show." Guide your child through rehearsal to build her confidence and review table manners if a formal meal is involved.

TIPS FOR 'TWEENS

In planning parties for your child, always stress the responsibility to serve guests. Encourage him to choose gifts for those attending and plan events with their preferences in mind. Teach him to be the kind of host friends will still like long after the party is over!

Everyone loves a party! If it is your child's party, involve her in planning what food, party favors, and games her guests might enjoy—not just what she wants. Serve guests politely and thank them for any gifts. If your child attends a party, remind her to give the party child and his parents a heartfelt "thank you!" when leaving.

Kids love the chance to use newly learned manners during special times!

Treat service workers with respect.

key point
GOOD MANNERS ARE A PATH TO MINISTRY.

Manners in public are especially important when it comes to service workers and other employees at restaurants, stores, and banks. Help your child realize these people deserve their best manners. Look for ways to show kindness through patience, polite words, and courteous behavior. Encourage your child to treat each person who serves him with honor and friendliness.

Friendly attitudes encourage good service. Teach your child to look at the server's nametag if he has one and to say hello. Always use please and thank you and tell the server when he is doing a good job, especially if he seems frazzled. Finally, leave your table and surrounding area picked up and be sure your napkins are placed beside your plates.

TARGET MOMENT

Leaving a tip is a prime opportunity to bless someone and reward their work. Avoid leaving gospel pamphlets instead of tips. This will more likely cause the waiter to disdain Christians as preachy—and cheap.

Model good shopping behavior by speaking to clerks with a smile and trying to understand when circumstances are out of their control. Mannerly behavior and a smile can be the best encouragement for service workers on tough days! Remind your child that Jesus taught us to serve others—and as clerks try to serve us the best they can, we can serve them with encouraging smiles!

Teach your child the importance of polite actions and a pleasant approach while discussing appropriate boundaries for his own safety. Chat about how to be polite and pleasant without being too friendly. It's important to nurture polite behavior and wisdom in our children without spoiling their desire to reach out to others.

Challenge your child to find a kind way to compliment each service worker you meet. A happy "You have a nice smile" or "I hope your day is bright" works wonders—and encourages your child to look for good in everyone!

Show good manners with friends.

To build healthy, meaningful, lasting friendships, children need to practice social manners that continue to model the biblical standard of "considering others first."

"Please" and "thank you" make friendships.

key point
SHARING AND FORGIVING ARE FRIEND-MAKERS.

No one can get along for very long with a friend who is grabby, selfish, or self-centered. "Gimme" isn't a word that will keep a friendship strong. It's important for your child to learn that he is not the center of the universe and will need to communicate his needs verbally rather than "muscling" others to get his way.

Find joy in generosity! Your child will love seeing you surprise others with a smile!

- **Pay for someone at a toll booth.**
- **Leave your change at a fast-food window for the next customer's tab.**
- **Give a child an extra quarter for a ride at the store.**

Friendships during the growing-up years are often on-again, off-again relationships, but they set the stage for friendships that last longer as your child matures and learns to express himself in mannerly, polite ways. Be observant and involved when your child needs to apologize to a friend or sibling or when he needs to offer forgiveness.

Discuss the following quotes about friendship with your child. How does being polite and thoughtful help us in our relationships?

"The only way to have a friend is to be one."
—Ralph Waldo Emerson

"A friend loves at all times."
—Proverbs 17:17

Good manners open the door to being—and having—good friends! Talk to your child about basic "kid" manners such as not cutting in line, letting someone use the water fountain first, not insisting on the largest cookie, or picking up an item someone else dropped. Role-play different situations to help your child choose how to act politely and with good manners.

Remember: Your child learns about friends from your examples. Do you talk openly about being wronged by others or show obvious disdain for someone you need to forgive? Ask God to make you aware of friendships that need attention and to keep your friendships healthy.

Help your child take opportunities to minister to friends who are ill with get-well notes. Encourage your child to phone a friend who missed school, assist a friend with his chores, share a piece of candy, or help shop for his birthday present. Remind your child that good friends are hard to find and should be handled with caring manners!

TIPS FOR 'TWEENS

Sing the camp classic "Make New Friends" with your child. Discuss what the song teaches us about friendships and how manners play a role.

Make new friends
But keep the old—
One is silver
And the other's gold!

Visiting others requires our best behavior.

TARGET MOMENT

Bringing a gift for a host or hostess is a wonderful practice that honors the host and models generosity and kindness.

As guests, we realize the people we visit are gracious to share their homes and we go by their house rules. We respect when they want to eat, if they watch TV or not, and whether or not they wear shoes in the house. As long as no moral rule is being violated, a good guest goes along with the house practices of the family hosting the visit.

If your child accompanies you to visit an adult friend with no children, expect your child to have a good, friendly attitude, but also allow your child to bring a book or project to work on as you visit. Remind your child that good manners include not touching things around the house, chasing the family's pet, asking too many questions, or wandering off.

TIPS FOR 'TWEENS

As a special thank-you for a spending the night with a friend, allow your older child to choose or design a thank-you note of her own. Remind her to tuck one into her sleep-over bag—it's fun to leave a note behind on the pillow of a neatly made bed!

key point
GOOD GUESTS RESPECT THEIR HOSTS.

key point
GRAND-PARENTS ARE HOSTS, TOO!

Children should respect property by walking in the house, taking off dirty shoes before stepping on floors, and playing carefully with a friend's toys. For an overnight stay, teach your child to place dirty clothes back in his bag and put his bathroom items in his bag after use, keeping the host's home neat and tidy. Remind your child to express his thanks when the visit is over.

No one likes to be taken for granted. You may see grandparents often, but your child should still greet them cheerfully. And no matter how comfortable we are in their houses, remind your child that it's common courtesy to ask before using anything or getting snacks out of the refrigerator! Of course, at Grandma's there's usually a filled cookie jar—but remind your child to politely ask first!

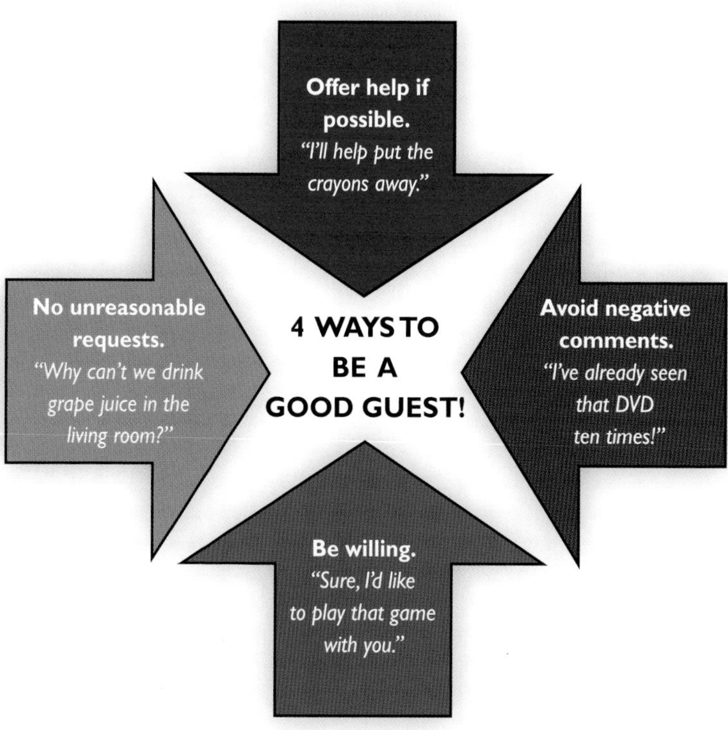

4 WAYS TO BE A GOOD GUEST!
Offer help if possible.
"I'll help put the crayons away."
No unreasonable requests.
"Why can't we drink grape juice in the living room?"
Avoid negative comments.
"I've already seen that DVD ten times!"
Be willing.
"Sure, I'd like to play that game with you."

Show good manners at church.

Different churches have different "personalities." Some may expect silence in a sanctuary, while others play celebrative music. No matter what behavior is expected, believers act out of a desire to show respect for other worshipers—and for God!

Express respect for God.

key point
RESPECT GOD'S HOUSE—THE CHURCH.

Respect for God is nurtured and cultivated all through our lives. It's important for your child to realize that when we respect God by worshiping at church, the best way we can honor Him is by participating actively—not just as sitting spectators. When a hymn is sung, a prayer prayed, or a sermon shared, we should pay attention to discover what God wants to teach us.

Depending on your child's age, it may be difficult for her to sit through a full adult service and sermon. Younger children may need a coloring page during adult sermons. Do encourage your child to pray along with the congregation, participate in singing, and follow along in Bible readings, if she can read. These are all ways to respect God and the congregation.

TIPS FOR TODDLERS

Kids under three have a hard time sitting through adult worship. If your church has a nursery or preschool program, this is a better place for your little ones!

As your child begins to struggle with peer pressure, remind her often that church is an opportunity to focus on God while we enjoy family and friends who don't compete for popularity. Don't allow church to become a fashion show or talent contest. Remind your child that clothes that draw attention to themselves have no place in a worship setting, where God should be the central focus.

In the Old Testament, the tabernacle in the desert was a very holy tent that only the priests could enter. Read Exodus 40 and discuss the following:

- *Who could go into the tabernacle?*
- *Who can enter our church today?*
- *How does acting politely in church honor God? show respect for other people in church?*

Draw your family into a unified, active-faith experience instead of just performing a Sunday "duty."

key point
HONOR GOD BY LISTENING IN CHURCH.

Respect for the church building shows respect for God. Encourage your child to look for ways to help with church housekeeping, such as straightening Bibles and planting flowers around the building. Respect also includes walking instead of running and using "indoor voices." Clearly communicate to your child what is expected of him when it comes to respecting God and the particular church building where the family worships.

Express respect for your church family.

Respect for God is shown not only by the way we treat the worship building but by the way we treat others who are in that building! Greet the church staff and members with courtesy and welcome visitors with polite smiles and an extension of friendship. We respect our church family by taking time to be interested in their lives, which means we need good listening skills.

Encourage your child to defer to the older members of the congregation by taking opportunities to hang up coats, open doors, or serve them in any way. Discourage unsupervised tearing around the building that might become a distraction to others preparing for worship. Limit time before and after church to quietly chatting or sharing with friends.

BIG BIBLE POINT

Read Colossians 3:15 with your child and discuss the following:

- *How does respecting others in church honor Jesus?*
- *As a church family, how can we demonstrate compassion, thoughtfulness, and polite manners?*
- *What are ways you can express your respect to others in church this week?*

key point

MODEL JESUS TO YOUR CHURCH FAMILY.

Roughly seven out of ten American adults (71%) regularly attended a Christian church during their childhood.

(George Barna, 1997)

PARENTS POINTER

It's important to teach children to honor the elderly members of society, especially if you don't have grandparents nearby. Relationships with older adults open doors between generations.

key point
GREET OTHERS WARMLY.

key point
BE CONSIDERATE AT CHURCH EVENTS.

At special events such as potlucks, insist that your child allow elder members of the congregation to be served first. Keep your child with you in the food line and guide him in using serving utensils and taking reasonable portions. Have your child help with cleanup, whether he clears his own plate or wipes off tables after the event.

Communicate to your child how she should address your minister or church leader. Your child shows respect for the pastor and for God by honoring your pastor. Teaching your child how to treat church members with respect will lead him into being able to give others the same polite preference and deference outside of church.

"Respect for ourselves guides our morals; respect for others guides our manners."
— Laurence Sterne

HOW GOOD MANNERS BEHAVE!

Use this helpful chart to give you a good idea of what general manners kids need to nurture in these different situations.

AT HOME

- Use "please" and "thank you" liberally.
- Help out around the house with chores.
- Look for ways to encourage one another.
- Steer clear of fights and arguments.
- Respect other people's privacy at home.
- Clean up messes before being asked.
- Look at others when they speak.
- Be a good listener.

REMEMBER: MANNERS ARE AS IMPORTANT AT HOME AS THEY ARE AWAY. GOOD MANNERS COUNT ALL THE TIME!

AS A HOST OR HOSTESS

- Welcome your guests warmly.
- Put out a clean guest towel in the bathroom.
- Offer your guest the best treats.
- Serve your guest first.
- Make your guests feel "at home."
- Defer to your guests and their wishes.
- Thank your guests for visiting.

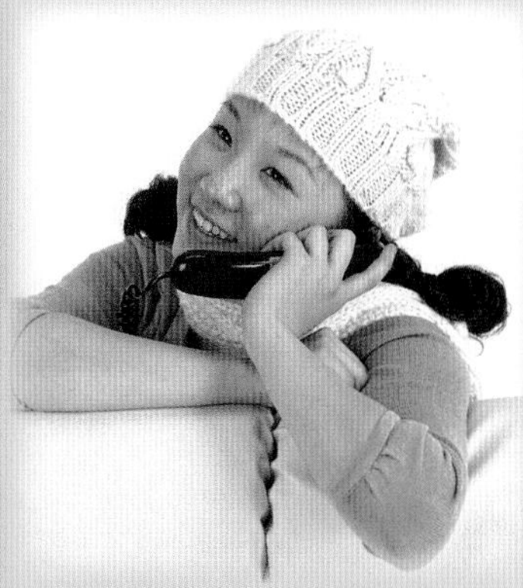

AT MEALTIME

- Wash before eating.
- Serve others first.
- Chew with your mouth closed.
- Wipe your mouth often.
- Pass dishes to the right.
- Knives go to the right of the plate.
- Spoons go to the right of knives.
- Speak in pleasant voices.
- Keep chat nice at the table.
- Keep elbows off of the table.
- Sit up straight; don't fidget.
- Sit quietly while others are eating.
- Compliment the cook.
- Take small helpings.
- Take small bites.
- Place your napkin on your lap.
- Say "please" and "thank you."
- Forks go left of the plate.

MANNERS MAKE MEALTIME FUN FOR EVERYONE!

AT CHURCH

- Sit quietly and don't fidget.
- Greet others with a smile.
- Listen to the sermon.
- Join in the songs and prayers.
- Offer to help straighten Bibles or hymnals.
- Whisper if you need to speak.
- Respect the church building.
- Be considerate of other worshipers.
- Respect God.

POLITE MANNERS SHOW WE HONOR GOD AND OTHERS.

WHILE VISITING OTHERS

- Thank your host for inviting you.
- Say "please" and "thank you."
- Don't run in the house.
- Don't snoop!
- Don't touch things without permission.
- Use polite table manners.
- Help your host clean up or pick up.
- Write thank-you notes for overnight visits.

SPECIAL OCCASIONS REQUIRE SPECIAL MANNERS.

AT WEDDINGS

- Sit still without wiggling.
- Smile and be pleasant.
- Don't talk during the wedding ceremony.
- Offer the bride and groom your best wishes.
- Don't run at the reception.
- Take a small amount of food.
- Offer to help clean up.

AT FUNERALS

- Sit quietly and respectfully.
- Speak softly if you need to speak at all.
- Use kind, caring expressions and words.
- Use tissues if you need to.

How We Treat Others

Loving others and showing them the love of Jesus is what being a Christian is all about. When we think about others and place their wants and needs before our own, we model Jesus' heart of love and servanthood in action!

Good manners require grace.

Discourtesy is everywhere in our busy, self-centered culture. We need to be equipped with grace and an attitude that allows us to behave politely in the face of others' shortcomings.

Be gracious when others are rude to you.

Have you ever met a person who interrupted you at work without thinking before he spoke? Did you keep working in hopes he'd quietly go away, did you become more irritated with every moment, or did you smile and say politely, "I'm sorry, but I can't chat now." Basic courtesy even in the face of carelessness or thoughtlessness is what good manners are all about!

Patience is a difficult virtue to master. Read 1 Thessalonians 5:14-18 with your child and answer these questions about patience and other virtues.

- *With whom are we to be patient?*
- *Why is it wrong to pay back rude behavior with more rude behavior?*
- *How does forgiveness help us have patience when dealing with rude or hurtful behavior?*

Help your child understand that it's vital to take responsibility for ourselves and our own behavior—and that choosing to be polite even when others act rudely not only keeps our own anger in check but also diffuses rude situations quickly. Good manners improve situations for everyone; complaining never helps.

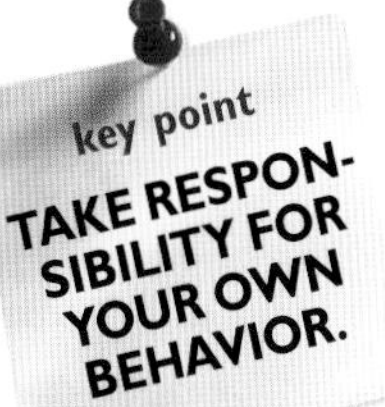

key point
TAKE RESPON-
SIBILITY FOR
YOUR OWN
BEHAVIOR.

TRY THIS!

To overcome the rudeness of pointing out others' mistakes, "police" each other in a positive way. Tonight at the dinner table, assign someone to "catch" others in the act of good manners. Take turns finding good manners and polite behavior. Manners that are praised will multiply!

Explain the concept of grace and how to walk away and forgive, not allowing the situation to escalate into an argument. It's important for your child to develop the ability to evaluate his own behavior, to overlook others' shortcomings, and to forgive mistakes instead of pointing them out.

"The test of good manners is to be able to put up pleasantly with bad ones."
—Wendell L. Willkie

Patience to deal with others' shortcomings takes time. Talk about thoughtless actions and situations that arise and how they were managed well or could be handled better. Make forgiveness a part of your family's daily devotional time. Evaluate your behavior and responses to others, then ask God to lead you into a new attitude of grace and forgiveness.

Be gracious when others are kind to you.

key point
EXPRESS KINDNESS WITH "THANK YOU."

Kids often find themselves at a loss of how to respond to positive words or kind actions. But part of being gracious is being able to receive compliments and help with joyful gratitude. When your child feels embarrassment at compliments or acts of kindness, remind him that God shines through others into our lives by bringing kindness, for which we can express our thanks politely and warmly.

Tell your child that the simplest, best way to receive a compliment is by saying "thank you." Don't over-analyze others' attempts to be kind. Help your child understand that when she's complimented or is treated kindly, she can show her gratitude by saying "thank you." If a compliment is voiced in an uncomfortable or less-than-polite manner, receive it and move on in the same way—don't make it an opportunity for a disagreement.

I luve you mom
and dad

"Toddler compliments" come in interesting packages. But busy parents may miss a tug on the pant leg or an adoring look that says "I love you!" These simple expressions pass by too quickly. Don't allow your schedule to crowd them out!

Kindness should be recognized not only in special cases but in the everyday events of family life. Model responses to kindness whether you receive a bouquet on your birthday or a cute drawing from your toddler. Encourage your child to express appreciation with a smile, a "thank you," a hug—or by reciprocating with her own act of kindness. Remember: The two words "thank you" cannot be expressed enough!

If it is proper to thank other people who give us good gifts and acts of kindness, how much more so should we thank God for daily blessings? Help your child name some of the blessings, gifts, and grace God provides and of the very great price Christ paid that we might receive His love. Live with gratitude and humble willingness to receive and thank God for His gifts!

If you receive a compliment from your spouse or child, a hug and a loving "thank you" are in order no matter what you're doing. Model the beauty of gracious thank-yous!

Good manners reflect our love for God.

As we care for others and place them before us, our love for them and for God is reflected through our manners.

Kind manners accept others.

key point
APPRECIATE THE DIVERSITY OF LIFE.

"I praise you because I am fearfully and wonderfully made" (Psalm 139:14). God created human beings as uniquely as flowers. And because God values each individual, we must do the same. Good manners leave no room for teasing or leaving others out because they are "different." It's important for your child to realize that accepting individuals and their differences means accepting their warts along with their wonders!

key point
RESPECT OTHERS' INDIVIDU-ALITY.

BIG
BIBLE
POINT

Kids love the story of Jesus and Zacchaeus from Luke 19:1-10. After reading it aloud, discuss the importance of accepting others.

- *Why do you think Jesus accepted Zacchaeus?*
- *What happened after Jesus accepted Zacchaeus?*
- *What can we learn about accepting others from this story?*
- *Who is someone you can accept this week?*

Children are naturally curious, so your child may stare at someone in a wheelchair or a person with a mental disorder. Quietly and gently direct your child to look at you, then explain that it hurts others' feelings to stare. Explain that those who suffer disabilities deserve the same respect as those without them and that they too are wonderfully made!

As you teach your child about accepting others, include a discussion about prejudice or stereotypes. Explain that "prejudice" means an unfounded dislike of someone simply because of what they look like, how they worship, or how much money they have. Talk about why prejudice sets up walls against accepting others and how God accepts everyone with loving arms!

PARENTS POINTER

Take time to introduce your child to other ways of life. Rent a movie set in another country. Attend a local Special Olympics. Learn sign language. When you accept and celebrate others who are different, you teach your child to respect others—and God!

Kids need to realize that if we separate ourselves from others instead of accepting and getting to know them, we're the ones who miss out. We also close the door to practicing unity by getting to know and appreciate someone who is different from us—and that door may be the way through which someone is introduced to Jesus!

Use the Internet or books to learn about people of a different culture. Make paper figures of those people and list foods and traditions on the backs of the figures. Share your exciting finds with the entire family!

Cuddle with your child and thumb through the pages of a magazine as you point out different people and what makes them alike (smiles, facial features, nice eyes) and what makes them different (ages, hair color, expressions, gender). Chat with your child about what it means to accept others for who they are—and why it's nice that God accepts us! Remind your child that God looks at our hearts, not our outward appearances.

Kind manners forgive others.

TRY THIS!

Make a set of Family Forgiveness Spoons. Use permanent markers to draw happy faces on spoons, then glue on cards that say "Forgive me," "You're forgiven," and "I'm sorry." Add self-adhesive magnets and stick the spoons on the refrigerator. When someone needs to ask or offer forgiveness, present a spoon to that person. Use the spoons over and over as needed!

TIPS FOR 'TWEENS

Explain the concept of grace by encouraging your 'tween to show grace toward younger siblings who seem like pests. Remind them of the grace shown toward them when they were young.

As we remember not to focus on the faults of others, we will be called upon again and again to practice biblical forgiveness. We may long for others to act out of courtesy, but they may not. When your child encounters rude behavior, he must be taught the art of forgiving others over and over (forgiving "seventy times seven" times) as many times as he is hurt or offended.

It's not easy for children to understand or accept that forgiveness must be shown over and over. But if we're to reflect Jesus' love to others, then forgiveness must be politely, if not easily, offered. Forgiveness is not easy, but remind your child that it's best to forgive quickly and not "score-keep" or hold on to wrongs committed. Staying angry or irritated only hurts the one who refuses to forgive.

key point
USE
SINCERE
APOLOGIES.

Ephesians 4:26 teaches us not to let the sun go down while we are still angry. Your child will not be able to sleep well if he's angry or knows someone is angry with him. Forgive one another before the sun goes down—or hopefully before! Show grace to your child as Jesus shows grace to you. Help your child realize that life is too short to waste on nurturing grudges, especially toward family members.

key point
FORGIVE
TO BE
FORGIVEN.

BIG BIBLE POINT

Read aloud the parable of the Unmerciful Servant from Matthew 18:21-35 to your child, then ask each other the following questions.

- *Am I quick to be irritated by others' bad manners, or do I forgive faults immediately? Explain.*
- *Do I take rudeness as a personal offense or chalk it up to human nature and go on? Explain.*
- *Is it as easy to accept as well as offer forgiveness? Explain.*

Psalm 103:12 states, "As far as the east is from the west, so far has he removed our transgressions from us." When God forgives us, He doesn't keep score—He forgets our sins. Read this verse aloud to your child, then ask Jesus to help you let go of any grudges so that bitterness doesn't take root. Help your child realize that "inner manners" of the heart are some of the most important manners we can have!

Kind manners share with others.

key point
SHARE SINCERELY AND WILLINGLY.

key point
SHARING IS GOOD STEWARDSHIP.

TRY THIS!

One of the hardest times to share may be at the family dinner table! Make a rule that each person must serve someone else before he serves himself to encourage sharing and thinking of others first.

The word "mine" tends to be learned early in life and is repeated by toddlers and preschoolers quite liberally! Sharing means giving up a portion of what we have when our human natures demand we keep things for ourselves. As Christians, we know God is the true owner of everything and that we are just borrowers of what is already His. In other words, when we share with others, we share what really belongs to God!

Ask your child what ways he can share. Perhaps he can share an encouraging word with a friend or lend a listening ear to someone with troubles. He can share food or clothing with the needy or share time by helping an ill neighbor walk his dog. Remind your child that sharing our material possessions is important, but sharing and giving of ourselves is best of all!

TARGET MOMENT

Proverbs 22:9 says, "A generous man will himself be blessed, for he shares his food with the poor." Ask your child what this verse teaches us about being generous instead of stingy or greedy.

Before your child can understand and apply kind manners that share with others outside of the home, he needs to experience sharing and sacrifice within his own family. Try sharing chores, games, or a fun time at the zoo! And don't forget to share your time with your child even though you may be too tired for a story or game of catch. Help your child see that caring and sharing go hand-in-hand and can offer loads of fun through loving attention and communication!

key point
SHARING BEGINS AT HOME.

Having an attitude of giving begins in the heart and comes out in our actions. Explain to your child that he can grudgingly split the last piece of chocolate cake with his sister or see an opportunity to cheerfully offer the whole piece. Sharing out of obligation meets a need but doesn't allow us to become more like Christ. As your child shares freely and sincerely, he will begin to realize a small part of what Christ sacrificed for us!

TOO BUSY TO CARE?

"Not now—I'm busy!" Do you avoid sharing your time and attention? Make it a point to interrupt tasks for hugs, a listening ear, a word of comfort, or a funny joke!

COFFEE BREAK

- **How do my own attitudes of sharing affect my child?**
- **Do I willingly share my time? belongings? love?**
- **Do I share with my family as easily as with others?**
- **When did I last share with my child or family?**

Kind manners put others first.

Kind manners look for opportunities to put others first who are even more in need than we are: the frazzled mom trying to gather her kids together at the local pizza hangout, the grandmother in the grocery line with all her coupons, or the dad in line at the post office who needs a break. Reminders to kindly and compassionately put others first are important for everyone!

MANNERS ALWAYS TAKE TURNS.

Kids need to learn that putting others first also means placing their own needs behind the needs of others as Jesus did. It means being a servant to all and living Jesus' truth that the first shall be last and the least will be the greatest (Luke 9:48). Putting others first may mean opening a door for someone, but it also means acting in selfless ways.

PARENTS POINTER
As a parent, you're probably used to being placed second, third, or even fourth in the family. Make time to be good to yourself, too.
• Go out for coffee with a friend.
• Get a massage.
• Plan a date with your spouse.
• Take a long bubble bath.

Our driving habits say a lot about our manners! Be careful how you speak and react to other drivers and how you let them (or don't let them) turn or go ahead of you. Your child needs to see you putting others first all the time—even when you're in the car!

Jesus was God Himself but gave up His right to "go first" in a huge way. The King became the servant of all; the greatest became the least in order to serve. In a world that world constantly screams "Me first!" and "Look out for number one," Jesus willingly and compassionately put us first. When you help your child look at putting others before him in this way, it allows him to serve others out of a heart grateful for Jesus' sacrifice!

key point

SERVE ALL AS JESUS SERVED.

Your preschooler can open doors for others and invite them to go ahead of her. Persuade your older child to allow another family member to choose the first cookie or slice of pizza. These small but powerfully effective opportunities build a firm foundation of seeking ways to put others first. But remember: You may need to let some of those drivers in ahead of you if you want to set a good example!

Kind manners respect adults and elders.

It's a sad fact that Americans do not honor their elderly as many other cultures do. Though not dishonored, older folks often become ignored. What a wealth of love and experience the generations can share when we approach each other with open hearts and respect! Kids need to realize that we'll all be grown-ups and "elders" one day, so it's wise to set an example by honoring them now!

Read Leviticus 19:32, then discuss the following questions about respecting our elders:

- *Who is talking to us in this verse?*
- *What three things does God tell us to do in this verse?*
- *Why is it vital to respect adults and the elderly?*
- *What can you learn from older people?*
- *How can you honor those who are elderly?*

Teach your child how to address those who are older than himself at church with a polite "good morning" using their proper title and surname. For example, it's more polite and respectful for your child to say "Good morning, Mrs. Anderson" than to say "Hi, Sarah." Unless otherwise told, any grown-up should be addressed using a proper title and surname.

Kind manners show respect for elders—and our commitment to honoring God!

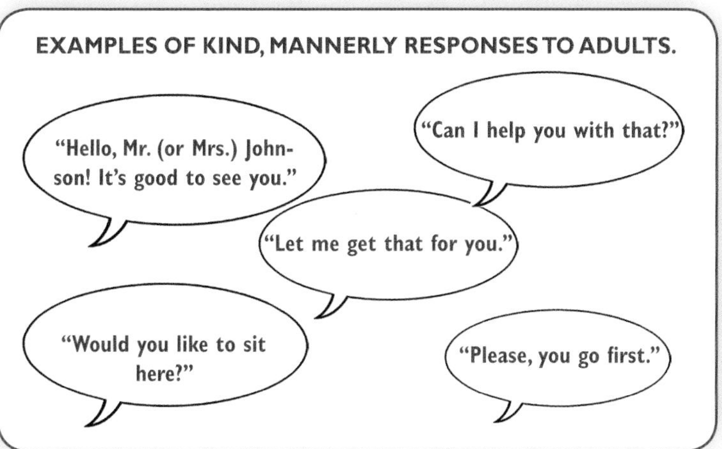

EXAMPLES OF KIND, MANNERLY RESPONSES TO ADULTS.
"Hello, Mr. (or Mrs.) Johnson! It's good to see you."
"Can I help you with that?"
"Let me get that for you."
"Would you like to sit here?"
"Please, you go first."

key point
HONOR THOSE OLDER THAN YOU.
key point
LISTENING SHOWS RESPECT.

Today it seems as though many families have tossed aside the policy of children being "seen and not heard." Kids often need many reminders not to interrupt, but waiting their turn to talk shows respect for adults and elderly people. This is not an offense to the child when it is done in a loving and affirming manner—it is part of your role in guiding him and teaching him to respect adults.

There are several basic ways you can help your child show respect for adults and seniors. Standing when an adult enters the room is one simple way. Another is to greet and show genuine interest in someone who is older. Your child isn't too young to ask "How are you?" and be sincere in wanting to know! Remind your child that good listening skills demonstrate respect—and with the interesting stories most older people have, your child may be enriched in delightful ways!

Good manners affect our lives in many ways.

When we learn how to treat others with consideration, compassion, and respect, we interact with confidence and become more effective with communication.

Being polite and kind brings others near.

When we're kind and considerate of others, there's no doubt about it—people are drawn to us! And reminding your child that, when we supply what people need, we're truly servants of the Lord. Who can resist a friend who is kind and considerate? Manners are one of the ways to show the kind of heart and behavior that draws others like a magnet!

PARENTS POINTER

Consider your family's mindset: Do you reach out to others or do things mostly for the benefit of your own family? Do you tend to be self-centered or a bit prideful? Work to become the kind of family that draws others near.

key point
GOOD MANNERS PLEASE PEOPLE.

Ask your child why he dislikes or is frustrated by certain people. Then ask him what he likes about a friend. Compare and contrast the relationships and point out that good manners and polite behavior are probably best exemplified through his good friend. Remind your child that to have a friend he must be a good friend—and to have good friends takes good manners and polite behavior from us!

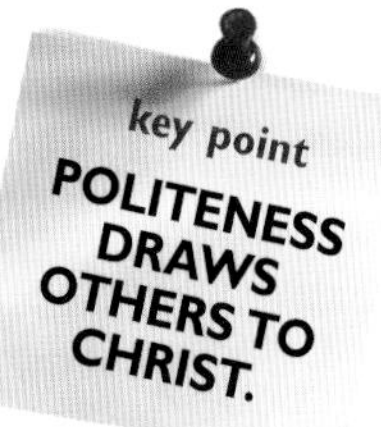
key point
POLITENESS DRAWS OTHERS TO CHRIST.

TIPS FOR TODDLERS

Provide crackers and slices of fruit for snacking, then invite your toddler to serve the snacks to family members as she reaches out through kind, polite sharing!

Chat with your child about what the world would be like if everyone acted selfishly and with poor manners. Help your child understand that poor manners and self-centered behavior is a "turn-off" to most people but that kind, considerate behavior encourages others to like us. Remind your child that when we show kind manners to others, we make Jesus known to them!

In your family's devotional times or mealtimes, add a simple "manners reminder" every day. Try challenging the whole family to use a specific manner such as opening the door for someone, then following through by using that manner during the week. Chat about how others respond when polite manners are shown.

Draw up a simple contract as a family that all of you can sign. Commit to simple efforts toward improved manners and reaching out. Then check the contract next month to see how you're doing!

Being respectful and reverential brings us near God.

key point
MANNERS HONOR GOD.

Manners, etiquette, and polite behavior may seem to your child like simple, silly, nagging lessons of life—but they are so much more! Behind every manner is a motive, and behind every polite action is an attitude. Motives and attitudes that encourage us to treat others as we want to be treated come from God. When we do not respect God or others, we cannot please Him or enjoy His blessings.

Take a moment to reflect with your child about the blessings God has so richly given you. Offer a prayer of thanks for His grace and generosity. Then ask God to show you more ways to share and show your love through serving others.

key point
SELFLESSNESS DRAWS US TO GOD.

BIG BIBLE POINT

Read Romans 8:5-8, then ask the following questions about revering God.

- *What are the rewards of a life controlled by the Spirit?*
- *How are manners a part of being controlled by the Spirit?*
- *What is impossible for someone who allows his sinful nature to control him?*
- *How can you draw closer to God by being obedient?*

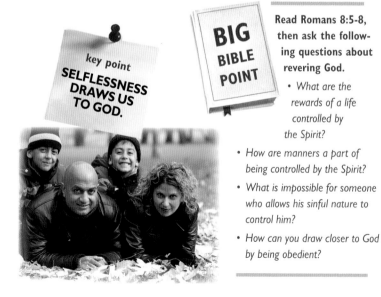

As your child begins to humbly reflect on God's great kindness in her life, she will want to express gratitude to God—and her respect and reverence. Guide your child in her prayers to say, "Thank you, God" and "What can I do for you?" Expressing her thanks and a willing heart demonstrates her love for God and a willingness to show that love through serving others.

Respect and honor for God brings your child close to Him, into that special, intimate relationship where your child can express his devotion, adoration, and honor. These are the divine "manners" that delight our Father and bring life—both for us and for the children with whom we are entrusted!

TARGET MOMENT

Remind your child to treat God as God would treat him. After all, God is our loving "Abba" (Father). A child who understands respect for a parent will be able to link that example with respect for God.

TIPS FOR 'TWEENS

Purchase a small notebook and invite your child to write God a short letter each night to share her feelings, praises, needs, and thanks. Remind her that God wants us to honor and talk to Him each day!

key point

GOD DESIRES OUR HONOR.

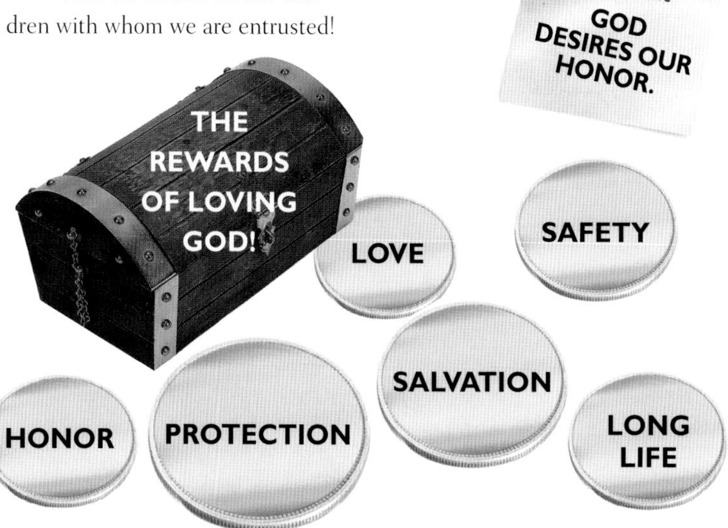

TREAT OTHERS RIGHT IN WORD & DEED

Use these helpful suggestions to give you a good idea of what you can say and do to treat others in mannerly and polite ways in various situations!

SITUATION	WHAT YOU CAN SAY	WHAT YOU CAN DO
Mealtime	"May I help with the dishes?"	Clear the table.
Mealtime	"Thank you for the great meal!"	Offer to wash the dishes.
At school	"Here, take one of my pencils."	Share school supplies with someone.
To someone ill	"I'm sorry you don't feel well. Can I help?"	Draw a get-well card or do a chore to help.
Loss of a game or competition	"Congratulations. You did a good job."	Shake hands.
After a fight with a friend	"I'm sorry. Will you forgive me?"	Give a hug.

SITUATION	WHAT YOU CAN SAY	WHAT YOU CAN DO
Answering an invitation	"I'd love to! Thanks!"	Send a thank-you note.
At a funeral	"I'm sorry. Is there anything I can do?"	Send a sympathy note or card.
At a wedding	"Congratulations and best wishes!"	Give a hug or a handshake.
Greeting an adult	"Hello, Mr. Smith (fill in title and name). How are you today?"	Give a handshake or smile.
After playing at a friend's house	"Thank you. I had fun!"	Smile; return the invitation to play.
Leaving a party	"Thank you for inviting me."	Handshake; send a thank-you card.
Helping an older person	"I'd be glad to help you."	Carry packages or run errands.
In a check-out line	"Please go ahead. We have time."	Smile; offer to step back.
To the Lord	"Thank you for Your blessings."	Pray; obey; serve others.

More Resources

BOOKS

for parents

- Sheryl Eberly, ***365 Manners Kids Should Know*** (Three Rivers Press, 2001).
- Judith Martin, ***Miss Manners' Guide to Rearing Perfect Children*** (Atheneum, 1984).
- Elizabeth L. Post, ***Emily Post's Etiquette*** (Funk and Wagnalls, 1960).
- Emilie Barnes, ***If Teacups Could Talk*** (Harvest House, 1994).

for children

- Nancy Holyoke and Debbie Tilley, ***Oops! The Manners Guide for Girls*** (American Girl Publishers, 1997).
- Emilie Barnes, ***A Little Book of Manners for Boys*** (Harvest House, 2000).
- Babette Cole, ***Lady Lupin's Book of Etiquette*** (Peachtree Publishers, 2002). Suitable for preschoolers.
- Aliki, ***Manners*** (Mulberry Books, 1997). Suitable for preschoolers.

RHYMING BOOKS TO ENJOY

- Jack Prelutsky, ***A Pizza the Size of the Sun*** (Greenwillow, 1996).
- Shel Silverstein, ***Where the Sidewalk Ends*** (HarperCollins Publishers, 1974).

DVDS

- ***The Berenstain Bears: Bears Mind Their Manners*** (Sony).
- ***Look Mom! I Have Good Manners*** (Available through the Web site at: www.WeBehave.com). Cool, interactive DVD to learn good manners with the character Willie Dooright.

WEBSITES

- **www.emilypost.com** (advice, books, articles, seminars, and discussions on etiquette)
- **www.lhj.com/home/Manners.html** (manners advice for all ages)
- **www.rudebusters.com/etikid.htm** (manners and activities for all ages)
- **www.smartkids101.com** (activities, games, and tips on manners)

Subpoint Index

Chapter 1: Manners Always Matter 8

Chapter 2: How We Speak 22

Chapter 3: How We Behave 46